World's

Humour

Oliver Roydhouse

The Five Mile Press

"If you can't celebrate,
what can you do...?"

– ATB

World's Best

Humour

The Five Mile Press

The Five Mile Press
22 Summit Road
Noble Park Victoria 3174
Australia

Published in 2000
All rights reserved

Collection Copyright © Oliver Roydhouse 2000

Editor: Sonya Plowman
Cover design: Sonia Juraja
Text design: Peter Bourne
Cover illustration: Ian Forss

Printed in Australia by Australian Print Group

National Library of Australia Cataloguing-in-Publication Data
Roydhouse, Oliver, 1977-.
World's best humour.

ISBN 1 86503 465 7

1. Wit and humor. 2. Joking. I. Title.
808.87

Cartoon Laws of Physics

Cartoon Law I

Any body suspended in space will remain in space until made aware of its situation.

A duck steps off a cliff, expecting further pastureland. He loiters in midair, soliloquising flippantly, until he looks down. At this point, the familiar principle of 10 metres per second takes over.

Cartoon Law II

Any body in motion will tend to remain in motion until solid matter intervenes suddenly.

Whether shot from a cannon or in hot pursuit on foot, cartoon characters are so absolute in their momentum that only a telephone pole or an oversized boulder retards their forward motion absolutely.

Cartoon Law III

Any body passing through solid matter will leave a perforation conforming to its perimeter.

Also called the silhouette of passage, this phenomenon is the speciality of victims of directed-pressure explosions and of reckless cowards who are so eager to escape that they exit directly through the wall of a house. The threat of skunks or matrimony often catalyses this reaction.

Cartoon Law IV

The time required for an object to fall 20 stories is greater than or equal to the time it takes for whoever knocked it off the ledge to spiral down 20 flights to attempt to capture it unbroken.

Such an object is inevitably priceless, the attempt to capture it inevitably unsuccessful.

Cartoon Law V

All principles of gravity are negated by fear.

Psychic forces are sufficient in most bodies for a shock to propel them directly away from the earth's surface. A spooky noise or an adversary's signature sound will induce motion upward, usually to the cradle of a chandelier, a treetop, or the crest of a flagpole. The feet of a character who is running or the wheels of a speeding auto need never touch the ground, especially when in flight.

Cartoon Law VI

As speed increases, objects can be in several places at once.

This is particularly true of tooth-and-claw fights, in which a character's head may be glimpsed emerging from the cloud of altercation at several places simultaneously. This effect is common as well among bodies that are spinning or being throttled. A 'wacky' character has the option of self-replication

6

only at manic high speeds and may ricochet off walls to achieve the velocity required.

Cartoon Law VII

Certain bodies can pass through solid walls painted to resemble tunnel entrances; others cannot.

This inconsistency has baffled generations, but at least it is known that whoever paints an entrance on a wall's surface to trick an opponent will be unable to pursue him into this theoretical space. The painter is flattened against the wall when he attempts to follow into the painting. This is ultimately a problem of art, not of science.

Cartoon Law VIII

Any violent rearrangement of feline matter is impermanent.

Cartoon cats possess even more deaths than the traditional nine lives might comfortably afford. They can be decimated, spliced, splayed, accordion-pleated, spindled, or disassembled, but they cannot be destroyed. After a few moments of blinking self-pity, the cartoon cats will re-inflate, elongate, snap back, or solidify.

Corollary: A cat will assume the shape of its container.

Cartoon Law IX

Everything falls faster than an anvil.

Cartoon Law X

For every vengeance there is an equal and opposite revengeance.

This is the one law of animated cartoon motion that also applies to the physical world at large. For that reason, we need the relief of watching it happen to a duck instead.

Cartoon Law Amendment A

A sharp object will always propel a character upward. When poked (usually in the buttocks) with a sharp object (usually a pin), a character will defy gravity by shooting straight up, with great velocity.

Cartoon Law Amendment B

The laws of object permanence are nullified for 'cool' characters.

Characters who are 'cool' can make previously non-existent objects appear from behind their backs at will. For instance, the Road Runner can materialise signs to express himself without speaking.

Cartoon Law Amendment C

Explosive weapons cannot cause fatal injuries. They merely turn characters temporarily black and smoky.

Cartoon Law Amendment D

Gravity is transmitted by slow-moving waves of large wavelengths.

Their operation can be witnessed by observing the behaviour of a canine suspended over a large vertical drop. Its feet will begin to fall first, causing its legs to stretch. As the wave reaches its torso, that part will begin to fall, causing the neck to stretch. As the head begins to fall, tension is released and the canine will resume its regular proportions until such time as it strikes the ground.

Cartoon Law Amendment E

Dynamite is spontaneously generated in 'C-spaces' (spaces in which cartoon laws hold).

The process is analogous to steady-state theories of the universe which postulated that the tensions involved in maintaining a space would cause the creation of hydrogen from nothing. Dynamite quanta are quite large (stick sized) and unstable (lit). Such quanta are attracted to psychic forces generated by feelings of distress in 'cool' characters (see Amendment B, which may be a special case of this law), who are able to use said quanta to their advantage. One may imagine C-spaces where all matter and energy result from primal masses of dynamite exploding. A big bang indeed.

Famous Last Words

I'll get a world record for this.

Let me reach in and get your watch out of the printing press.

Gee, that's a cute tattoo.

It's fireproof.

He's probably just hibernating.

What does this button do?

I'm making a citizen's arrest.

So, you're a cannibal.

It's probably just a rash.

Why am I standing on a plastic sheet?

Are you sure the power is off?

The odds of that happening have to be a million to one!

Pull the pin and count to what?

Which wire am I supposed to cut?

I wonder where the mother bear is.

I've seen this done on TV.

These are the good kind of mushrooms.

I'll hold it and you light the fuse.

Real Headlines

Something Went Wrong in Jet Crash, Expert Says

Panda Mating Fails; Veterinarian Takes Over

Police Begin Campaign to Run Down Jaywalkers

Safety Experts Say School Bus Passengers Should Be Belted

Drunk Gets Nine Months in Violin Case

Survivor of Siamese Twins Joins Parents

Iraqi Head Seeks Arms

Prostitutes Appeal to Pope

Include Your Children When Baking Cookies

British Left Waffles on Falkland Islands

Lung Cancer in Women Mushrooms

Eye Drops Off Shelf

Teachers Strike Idle Kids

Clinton Wins on Budget, But More Lies Ahead

Enraged Cow Injures Farmer With Axe

Plane Too Close to Ground, Crash Probe Told

Miners Refuse to Work After Death

Juvenile Court to Try Shooting Defendant

Stolen Painting Found by Tree

Two Sisters Reunited After 18 Years in Checkout Counter

Killer Sentenced to Die for Second Time in 10 Years

Never Withhold Herpes Infection From Loved One

War Dims Hope for Peace

If Strike Isn't Settled Quickly, It May Last a While

Cold Wave Linked to Temperatures

Deer Kill 17,000

Enfield's Couple Slain; Police Suspect Homicide

Red Tape Holds Up New Bridges

Typhoon Rips Through Cemetery; Hundreds Dead

Man Struck by Lightning Faces Battery Charge

New Study of Obesity Looks for Larger Test Group

Astronaut Takes Blame for Gas in Spacecraft

Kids Make Nutritious Snacks

Chef Throws His Heart into Helping Feed Needy

Arson Suspect Held in Massachusetts Fire

Ban on Soliciting Dead in Trotwood

Local High School Dropouts Cut in Half

New Vaccine May Contain Rabies

Hospitals Are Sued by 7 Foot Doctors

Things You Would Never Know Without the Movies

During all police investigations, it will be necessary to visit a strip club at least once.

When they are alone, all foreigners prefer to speak English to each other.

If being chased through town, you can usually take cover in a passing St Patrick's Day parade – at any time of year.

All beds have special L-shaped cover sheets which reach up to the armpit level on a woman but only to the waist level on the man lying beside her.

The chief of police will almost always suspend his star detective – or give him 48 hours to finish the job.

All grocery bags contain at least one stick of french bread.

The ventilation system of any building is the perfect hiding place – no one will ever think of looking for you in there and you can travel to any other part of the building undetected.

Police departments give their officers personality tests to make sure they are deliberately assigned to a partner who is their polar opposite.

The Eiffel Tower can be seen from any window in Paris.

All bombs are fitted with electronic timing devices with large red readouts so you know exactly when they are going to go off.

You are very likely to survive any battle in any war unless you make the mistake of showing someone a picture of your sweetheart back home.

Should you wish to pass yourself off as a German officer, it will not be necessary to speak the language – simply having a German accent will do.

A man will show no pain while taking the most ferocious beating but will wince when a woman tries to clean his wounds.

Kitchens don't have light switches. When entering a kitchen at night, you should open the fridge door and use that light instead.

If staying in a haunted house, women should investigate any strange noises in their most revealing underwear.

Cars that crash will almost always burst into flames.

Mediaeval peasants had perfect teeth.

Any person waking from a nightmare will sit bolt upright and pant.

Even when driving down a perfectly straight road, it is necessary to turn the wheel vigorously from left to right every few moments.

It is always possible to park directly outside the building you are visiting.

A detective can only solve a case once he has been suspended from duty.

It does not matter if you are heavily outnumbered in a fight involving martial arts – your enemies will patiently attack you one by one by dancing around in a threatening manner until you have knocked out their predecessors.

No one ever involved in a car chase, hijacking, explosion, volcanic eruption or alien invasion will ever go into shock.

Any lock can be picked by a credit card or a paper clip in seconds – unless it's the door to a burning building with a child trapped inside.

Television news bulletins usually contain a story that affects you personally at the precise moment that it is aired.

~~~~~~~~~

Make it idiot-proof and someone will make a better idiot.

Creative Ways to Say Someone is Stupid

He is depriving a village somewhere of its idiot.

Not the brightest bulb on the Christmas tree.

A few peas short of a casserole.

Fell out of the stupid tree and hit every branch on the way down.

An intellect rivalled only by garden tools.

Chimney's clogged.

Doesn't have all his dogs on one leash.

Elevator doesn't go all the way to the top floor.

Forgot to pay her brain bill.

Her sewing machine's out of thread.

His antenna doesn't pick up all the channels.

His belt doesn't go through all the loops.

Missing a few buttons on his remote control.

Not the sharpest knife in the drawer.

The wheel's spinning, but the hamster's dead.

She doesn't have all the chairs around the table.

She's not the brightest crayon in the box.

About as sharp as a marble.

The gates are down, the lights are flashing but the train isn't coming.

Fell out of the family tree.

Got into the gene pool while the lifeguard wasn't watching.

Insurance Claims

The following excuses are from actual insurance claim forms that are intended to concisely summarise the accident.

Coming home, I drove into the wrong house and collided with a tree I don't have.

The other car collided with mine without giving warning of its intentions.

I thought my window was down, but I found out it was up when I put my hand through it.

I collided with a stationary truck coming the other way.

A truck backed through my windshield into my wife's face.

A pedestrian hit me and went under my car.

The guy was all over the road, I had to swerve a number of times before I hit him.

I pulled away from the side of the road, glanced at my mother-in-law and headed over the embankment.

In my attempt to kill a fly, I drove into a telephone pole.

I had been shopping for plants all day and was on my way home. As I reached an intersection, a hedge sprang up, obscuring my vision.

I had been driving for 40 years when I fell asleep at the wheel and had an accident.

I was on my way to the doctor's with rear end trouble, when my universal joints gave way, causing me to have an accident.

As I approached the intersection, a stop sign suddenly appeared. It was too late to stop in time to avoid the accident.

To avoid hitting the bumper of the car in front, I struck the pedestrian.

My car was legally parked as it backed into the other vehicle.

An invisible car came out of nowhere, struck my car and vanished.

I told the police that I was not injured, but on removing my hat, I found that I had a skull fracture.

I was sure the old fellow would not make it to the other side of the street when I struck him.

The pedestrian had no idea which way to go, so I ran over him.

I saw the slow-moving, sad-faced gentleman as he bounced off the hood of my car.

I was thrown from my car as it left the road and I was later found in a ditch by some stray cows.

The telephone pole was approaching fast. I tried to swerve out of its way, when it struck the front of my car.

Warning Signs of Insanity

Your friends tell you that you have been acting strange lately, and then you hit them several times with a sledgehammer.

Everyone you meet appears to have tentacles growing out of places you wouldn't expect tentacles to be growing from.

You start out each morning with a 30-minute jog around the bathroom.

Every commercial you hear on the radio reminds you of death.

People stay away from you whenever they hear you howl.

You laugh out loud during funerals.

Nobody listens to you anymore, because they can't understand you through that scuba mask.

You begin to stop and consider all of the blades of grass you've stepped on as a child, and worry that their descendants are going to one day seek revenge.

You have meaningful conversations with your toaster.

Your father pretends you don't exist, just to play along with your little illusion.

You collect dead windowsill flies.

Whenever you listen to the radio, the music sounds backwards.

You have a predominant fear of fabric softener.

You wake up each morning and find yourself sitting on your head in the middle of your front lawn.

You tend to agree with everything your mother's dead uncle tells you.

You call up random people and ask if you can borrow their dog, just for a few minutes.

You argue with yourself about which is better: to be eaten by a koala or to be loved by an infectious disease.

You think that exploding wouldn't be so bad, once you got used to it.

People offer you help, but you unfortunately interpret this as a violation of your rights as a boysenberry.

You try to make a list of the Warning Signs of Insanity (cough).

Mathematics of Relationships

Smart man + smart woman = romance
Smart man + dumb woman = pregnancy
Dumb man + smart woman = affair
Dumb man + dumb woman = marriage
Smart boss + smart employee = profits
Smart boss + dumb employee = production
Dumb boss + smart employee = promotion
Dumb boss + dumb employee = overtime

~~~~~~~

Jesus is coming – quick, everybody look busy.

Women – A Chemical Analysis

Health and Safety Executive Hazardous Materials Report

ELEMENT: Woman

SYMBOL: Wo

DISCOVERER: Adam

ATOMIC MASS: Accepted as 53.6 kg but can range from 40-200 kg.

OCCURRENCE: Copious quantities in all urban areas.

Physical Properties

Boils at nothing, freezes with no known reason.

Melts if given special treatment.

Bitter if incorrectly used.

Found in various states, ranging from virgin metal to common ore.

Yields to pressure applied at correct points.

Chemical Properties

Has great affinity for precious metals and stones.

Absorbs great quantities of expensive substances.

May explode without warning, and with no known reason.

Insoluble in liquids, but activity greatly increases with saturation in alcohol.

Most powerful money-reducing agent known to man.

Common Uses
Highly ornamental – especially in the sun or a sports car.

Can be a great aid to relaxation.

Very effective cleaning agent.

Tests
Pure specimen turns rosy-pink when discovered in .natural state.

Turns green when placed beside a better specimen.

Potential Hazards

Highly dangerous, even in experienced hands.

Illegal to possess more than one, although several can be maintained in different locations so long as they do not come into direct contact with each other.

General Advice
Avoid contact wherever possible as cures can be expensive.

How to Be a Real Man

Don't call, ever.

If you don't like a girl, don't tell her. It's more fun to let her figure it out by herself.

Lie.

Name your penis. Be sure it is something narcissistic and unoriginal, such as 'spike'.

Use this pick-up line: 'My girlfriend's pregnant, will you go out with me?'

Play with yourself. Talk about it.

Be as ambiguous as possible. If you don't want to answer, a nice grunt will do.

Always remember: You are a man. Therefore, no matter what, it isn't your fault.

Lie.

Girls find it attractive if a man has had more women than baths.

Never ask for help. Even if you really, really need help – don't ask. People will think you have no penis.

Women like it when you ignore them. It arouses them.

Vanity is the most important trait for a man to have. Use reflective surfaces at every opportunity.

If, God forbid, you have to talk to a girl on the phone, use only monosyllabic words and noises. Bodily noises are permissible.

Hack and spit.

Everyone finds a man more attractive if he can write his name in urine.

One sure way to make a girl like you is to go after her best friend. She will then see what she's missing and love you for not giving up on her.

Tell her you will call. Then, refer back to rule #1.

Say things like 'Wha...?'

Don't wear matching clothes. People will think your girlfriend picked them out, and it will cramp your style when picking up chicks.

Lie.

Deny everything. Everything.

Use this break-up line: 'It's not me, it's you.'

If you like a girl, tell all your female friends about her.

Because if any of your female friends like you, they'll really want to know.

Don't have a clue.

If you get a clue, pretend you didn't and disregard it.

No means yes.

Yes means no.

If you don't get sex whenever you want, your balls will shrivel. Enforce this myth at all times.

If anyone asks, you have had sex in all possible positions and locations. Improvise.

Much like an orgasm signifies the end of a sexual peak, sex often signifies the end of a relationship.

Feelings? What feelings?

Life is one big competition. If someone is better than you at anything, either pretend it's not true or kick some arse.

Do not make decisions about relationships. If you are backed into a corner and must make a decision, stall.

If you still must come up with an answer, leave yourself a loophole for escape.

Every sentence that anyone says can be contorted to have sexual meaning. Do so.

At any given opportunity, point out how things look like various genitalia. If, by chance, you have Play-Doh, make sure you make an exact replica of your penis. Measure to make sure it's right.

Lie.

'Love' is not in your vocabulary. Don't even think about saying it.

A general rule: If whatever you're doing does not satisfy you completely in five minutes, it's really not worth it.

Dump your girlfriend. Beg and plead until you get her back. Dump her again. Repeat cycle.

Lie.

Always apologise. Never mean it.

If you hurt someone, pretend you care. Don't.

Try to have a good memory, but it's okay if you forget trivial things. You know, like your girlfriend's birthday and eye colour.

Ignorance solves problems. If you can't see them, they can't see you.

It is never your duty to take responsibility for your actions.

Create new words and phrases to describe genitalia, sex, semen etc.

Lie.

Play with your food only if you are in a public place with people you don't know.

Play with your penis only if you are in a public place with people you don't know.

If people express extreme disgust at whatever you are doing, don't stop! This is the desired reaction.

You are male, therefore you are superior.

Agenda for a boring evening: get beer. Drink beer. Play with yourself. Have sex. Drink more beer. Pass out.

Females do not care what you do to them as long as they get to please you.

Don't ever notice anything.

If you're going out with someone but you love someone else, don't say anything. Wait until the girl you are going out with falls in love with YOU, and then tell her.

Basic fundamental rule of dating: quantity, not quality.

Basic fundamental rule of sex: quantity *is* quality.

Lie.

If you cheat on a girl, but no one finds out, then technically you've done nothing wrong.

Crying is not manly. Then again, if you are a man, what do you have to cry about, anyway?

If the question begins with 'why' the answer is 'I don't know'.

Remember, every virgin girl is saving herself for YOU.

If you ever find yourself in a position where you have been proven wrong, blame others. Come up with creative and believable excuses why they are at fault – not you.

Don't ever let anyone say 'I told you so.' If you hear this phrase and it didn't come out of your mouth, go ballistic.

If your woman makes you go shopping with her, drive around until a parking spot right near the door opens up. If this takes hours, so be it. You will have the coveted 'door spot' and others will worship your skills.

Keep track of how many seconds in your life you have thought about sex. Compare with others.

If you do something really mean to a girl, and she doesn't want to talk to you, pretend nothing happened. If she still doesn't talk to you, casually ask, 'Is something wrong?'

Three words: let's be friends. Translation: I never want to speak to you again, but it's bad for my nice-guy image if you are mad at me, so I'll pretend I want to be your friend.

Lie.

If you're on a date, and there is a lull in the conversation, tell the girl how many different dorms you've been laid in.

Here's a good trick. Tell a girl that you're going to leave and when you come back, you want her naked, sprawled on the bed. Leave, and go into her dad's room and tell him that he should go check on his daughter.

Then drive like hell. (True story.)

The best sex position is you, lying face up... and twenty girls on top.

Practise your blank stare.

Spend your spare time thinking of excuses and shove them up your arse. Then, whenever you need one, you can pull it out of your arse.

If you are ever forced to show emotion, just pick random emotions like rage and lust and insanity and display them at random, inconvenient times. You won't be asked to do it again.

If you are asked to do something you really don't want to do, first try your manly best to get out of it. If that doesn't work, go ahead and do what you were asked to do, but complain that you don't know how to do it and continuously ask questions on how to do each little part. If still no one rushes in to do it for you, finish the job in the most half-arsed way you possibly can and then say, 'See? I told you I couldn't do it.' Eventually, people will stop asking you to do things.

Work out day and night to make your body even more beautiful than it already is. When people ask if you've been working out, say things like, 'No, Baby, I was born like this!'

Beer. Then more beer.

Dump your girlfriend for an occasional night or five out with 'the gang'.

Lie.

The Singles Bar

A collection of some of the worst pick-up lines of all time.

I may not be Fred Flintstone, but I bet I can make your Bed Rock.

I may not be the best-looking guy here, but I'm the only one talking to you.

If you're going to regret this in the morning, we can sleep until the afternoon.

Oh, I'm sorry, I thought that was a braille name tag.

Excuse me, do you have your phone number? I seem to have lost mine.

I'm new in town, could I have directions to your house?

You look like a girl that has heard every line in the book, so what's one more going to hurt?

F**k me if I'm wrong, but is your name Yolanda?

You might not be the most attractive girl here, but beauty is only a light switch away.

I lost my bed, can I borrow yours?

You must be Jamaican, because Jamaican me crazy.

Are your legs tired? Because you've been running through my mind all day long.

Hey baby, I'm like American Express, you don't want to leave home without me.

Do you have change? My mother told me to call home when I met the girl of my dreams.

The word for the night is legs – legs go back to my room and spread the word.

I can't find my puppy, can you help me find him? I think he went into this cheap motel room.

The fact that I'm missing my teeth just means that there's more room for your tongue.

Hi, my name is Pogo, want to jump on my stick?

~~~~~~~

Hard work has a future pay-off. Laziness pays off now.

Government Health Warnings

Due to increasing product liability litigation, wine, beer and spirit manufacturers have accepted the Medical Association's suggestion that the following warning labels be placed immediately on all containers...

Warning: consumption of alcohol may make you think you're whispering when you're not.

Warning: consumption of alcohol is a major factor in dancing like an idiot.

Warning: consumption of alcohol may cause you to tell the same boring story over and over again until your friends want to smash your head in.

Warning: consumption of alcohol may cause you to thay shings like thish.

Warning: consumption of alcohol may lead you to believe that ex-lovers are really dying for you to telephone them at four in the morning.

Warning: consumption of alcohol may leave you wondering what happened to your trousers.

Warning: consumption of alcohol may make you think that you can converse logically with members of the opposite sex without drooling.

Warning: consumption of alcohol may make you think that you have mystical Kung Fu powers.

Warning: consumption of alcohol may cause you to roll over in the morning and see something really scary (whose species and/or name you can't remember).

Warning: consumption of alcohol is the leading cause of inexplicable rug burns on the forehead.

Warning: consumption of alcohol may lead you to believe that you are invisible.

Warning: consumption of alcohol may lead you to believe that people are laughing *with* you.

Warning: consumption of alcohol may cause an influx in the time-space continuum, whereby small (and sometimes large) gaps of time may seem to literally disappear.

Warning: consumption of alcohol may cause pregnancy.

~~~~~~~~

I considered atheism but there weren't enough holidays.

~~~~~~~~

Learn from your parents' mistakes – use birth control!

English Subtitles to Hong Kong Movies

I am damn unsatisfied to be killed this way.

Fatty, you with your think face have hurt my instep.

Gun wounds again?

Same old rules: no eyes, no groin.

A normal person wouldn't steal pituitaries.

Damn, I'll burn you into a BBQ chicken!

Take my advice, or I'll spank you without pants.

Who gave you the nerve to get killed here?

Quiet you I'll blow your throat up.

You always use violence, I shouldn't have ordered the glutinous rice chicken.

I'll fire aimlessly if you don't come out!

You daring lousy guy.

Beat him out of recognisable shape!

I got knife scars more than the number of your leg's hair!

Beware! Your bones are going to be disconnected.

How can you use my intestines as a gift?

The bullets inside are very hot. Why do I feel so cold?

Personal Ad Translations

A list of abbreviations in the 'Women Seeking Men'
classifieds. The first word is the code word; the
second is the real meaning.

Adventurous = Has had more partners than you
ever will

Artist = Unreliable

Athletic = Flat-chested

Beautiful = Pathological liar

Contagious smile = Bring your own penicillin

Emotionally secure = Medicated

Enjoys art and opera = Snob

Exotic beauty = Would frighten a Martian

Feminist = Fat; ball buster

Free spirit = Substance user

Friendship first = Trying to live down reputation as
slut

Fun = Annoying

Gentle = Comatose

In transition = Needs new sugar-daddy to pay bills

Looks younger = If viewed from far away in bad light

Loves travel = If you're paying

Loves animals = Cat lady

Mature = Will not let you treat her like a farm animal in bed, like last boyfriend did

New-age = Hair all over

Old-fashioned = Lights out, missionary position only

Open-minded = Desperate

Poet = Depressive schizophrenic

Professional = Bitch

Redhead = Uses hair dye

Reubenesque = Hugely fat

Romantic = Looks better in candlelight

Self-employed = Jobless

Special = Took the short school bus

Spiritual = Involved with a cult

Tall, thin = Anorexic

Tanned = Wrinkled

Voluptuous = Very fat

Widow = Nagged first husband to death

Writer = Pompous

Young at heart = Toothless old fogey

Sniglets

Carperpetuation (kar' pur pet u a shun) n. The act, when vacuuming, of running over a string or a piece of lint at least a dozen times, reaching over and picking it up, examining it, then putting it back down to give the vacuum one more chance.

Disconfect (dis kon fekt') v. To sterilise the lolly you dropped on the floor by blowing on it, somehow assuming this will 'remove' all the germs.

Elbonics (el bon' iks) n. The actions of two people manoeuvring for one armrest in a movie theatre.

Elecelleration (el a cel er ay' shun) n. The mistaken notion that the more you press an elevator button the faster it will arrive.

Frust (frust) n. The small line of debris that refuses to be swept onto the dust pan. Finally the person gives up and sweeps it under the rug.

Lactomangulation (lak' to man gyu lay' shun) n. Manhandling the 'open here' spout on a milk container so badly that one has to resort to the 'illegal' side.

Peppier (pehp ee ay') n. The waiter at a fancy restaurant whose sole purpose seems to be walking around asking diners if they want ground pepper.

Phoneesia (fo nee' zhuh) n. The affliction of dialling a phone number and forgetting whom you were calling just as they answer.

Pupkus (pup' kus) n. The moist residue left on a window after a dog presses its nose to it.

Telecrastination (tel e kras tin ay' shun) n. The act of always letting the phone ring at least twice before you pick it up, even when you're only six inches away.

Actual Bumper Stickers

I love cats... they taste just like chicken.

Out of my mind. Back in five minutes.

Cover me. I'm changing lanes.

As long as there are tests, there will be prayer in public schools.

Laugh alone and the world thinks you're an idiot.

Sometimes I wake up grumpy; other times I let her sleep.

I want to die in my sleep like my grandfather... not screaming and yelling like the passengers in his car.

I didn't fight my way to the top of the food chain to be a vegetarian.

Your kid may be an honour student but you're still an idiot!

It's as bad as you think, and they *are* out to get you.

Smile, it's the second-best thing you can do with your lips.

Friends don't let friends drive naked.

Where there's a will, I want to be in it!

If we aren't supposed to eat animals, why are they made of meat?

Time is the best teacher; unfortunately it kills all its students!

It's lonely at the top, but you eat better.

Reality? That's where the pizza delivery guy comes from!

Warning: dates in calendar are closer than they appear.

Be nice to your kids. They'll choose your nursing home.

There are three kinds of people: those who can count and those who can't.

Ever stop to think, and forget to start again?

Diplomacy is the art of saying 'Nice doggie!'... till you can find a rock.

Two plus two equals five for extremely large values of two.

I like you, but I wouldn't want to see you working with subatomic particles.

I killed a six-pack just to watch it die.

Flight Attendants Can Be Humorous, Too

Occasionally, airline attendants make an effort to make the in-flight safety lecture and other announcements a bit more entertaining. Here are some real examples that have been heard or reported:

'Should the cabin lose pressure, oxygen masks will drop from the overhead area. Please place the bag over your own mouth and nose before assisting children or adults acting like children.'

'To operate your seatbelt, insert the metal tab into the buckle, and pull tight. It works just like every other seatbelt, and if you don't know how to operate one, you probably shouldn't be out in public unsupervised.'

'In the event of a sudden loss of cabin pressure, oxygen masks will descend from the ceiling. Stop screaming, grab the mask, and pull it over your face.'

'If you have a small child travelling with you, secure your mask before assisting with theirs. If you are travelling with two small children, decide now which one you love more.'

'Your seat cushions can be used for flotation, and in the event of an emergency water landing, please take them with our compliments.'

'Ladies and gentlemen, please remain in your seats with your seatbelts fastened while the captain taxis what's left of our aeroplane to the gate!'

'We'd like to thank you folks for flying with us today. And, the next time you get the insane urge to go blasting through the skies in a pressurised metal tube, we hope you'll think of us here.'

On a Lighter Note...

The following quotes are from actual medical records dictated by physicians:

By the time he was admitted, his rapid heart had stopped, and he was feeling better.

Patient has chest pain if she lies on her left side for over a year.

On the second day the knee was better and on the third day it had completely disappeared.

She has had no rigours or shaking chills, but her husband states she was very hot in bed last night.

The patient has been depressed ever since she began seeing me in 1983.

I will be happy to go into her GI system; she seems ready and anxious.

Patient was released to outpatient department without dressing.

I have suggested he loosen his pants before standing, and then, when he stands with the help of his wife, they should fall to the floor.

The patient is tearful and crying constantly. She also appears to be depressed.

Discharge status: alive without permission.

The patient will need disposition, and therefore we will get Mr Blank to dispose of him.

Healthy-appearing decrepit 69-year-old female, mentally alert but forgetful.

The patient refused an autopsy.

The patient has no past history of suicides.

The patient expired on the floor uneventfully.

Patient has left his white blood cells at another hospital.

Patient was becoming more demented with urinary frequency.

The patient's past medical history has been remarkably insignificant with only a 40-pound weight gain in the past three years.

She slipped on the ice and apparently her legs went in separate directions in early December.

The patient experienced sudden onset of severe shortness of breath with a picture of acute pulmonary oedema at home while having sex which gradually deteriorated in the emergency room.

Actual Answers Given by Contestants on *Family Feud*

Name something a blind person might use…
'A sword.'

Name a song with moon in the title…
'Blue suede moon.'

Name a bird with a long neck…
'Naomi Campbell.'

Name an occupation where you need a torch…
'A burglar.'

Name a famous brother and sister…
'Bonnie & Clyde.'

Name a dangerous race...
'The Arabs.'

Name an item of clothing worn by the three musketeers...
'A horse.'

Name something that floats in the bath...
'Water.'

Name something you wear on the beach...
'A deckchair.'

Name something red...
'My cardigan.'

Name a famous cowboy...
'Buck Rogers.'

Name a famous royal...
'Mail.'

Name a number you have to memorise...
'7.'

Name something you do before going to bed...
'Sleep.'

Name something you put on walls...
'Rooves.'

Name something in the garden that's green...
'Shed.'

Name something that flies that doesn't have an engine...

'A bicycle with wings.'

Name something you might be allergic to...
'Skiing.'

Name a famous bridge...
'The bridge over troubled waters.'

Name something a cat does...
'Goes to the toilet.'

Name something you do in the bathroom...
'Decorate.'

Name an animal you might see at the zoo...
'A dog.'

Name something associated with the police...
'Pigs.'

Name a sign of the zodiac...
'April.'

Name something slippery...
'A conman.'

Name a kind of ache...
'Fillet O' Fish.'

Name a food that can be brown or white...
'Potato.'

Name a jacket potato topping...
'Jam.'

Name a famous Scotsman...
'Jock.'

Name something with a hole in it...
'Window.'

Name a non-living object with legs...
'Plant.'

Name a domestic animal...
'Leopard.'

Name a part of the body beginning with 'n'...
'Knee.'

Name a way of cooking fish...
'Cod.'

Name something you open other than a door...
'Your bowels.'

Church Bulletins

The Scouts are saving aluminium cans, bottles and other items to be recycled. Proceeds will be used to cripple children.

The Outreach Committee has enlisted 25 visitors to make calls on people who are not afflicted with any church.

The pastor would appreciate it if the ladies of the congregation would lend him their electric girdles for the pancake breakfast next Sunday morning.

Low Self-esteem Group will meet Thursday at 7 pm. Please use the back door.

Ushers will eat latecomers.

For those of you who have children and don't know it, we have a nursery downstairs.

Reverend Merriwether spoke briefly, much to the delight of the congregation.

The pastor will preach his farewell message, after which the choir will sing 'Break Forth into Joy'.

A songfest was hell at the Methodist Church Wednesday.

Due to the rector's illness, Wednesday's healing service will be discontinued until further notice.

Remember in prayer the many who are sick of our church and community.

The eighth-graders will be presenting Shakespeare's *Hamlet* in the church basement Friday at 7 pm. The congregation is invited to attend this tragedy.

The concert held in Fellowship Hall was a great success. Special thanks are due to the minister's daughter, who laboured the whole evening at the piano which as usual fell upon her.

Don't let worry kill you. Let the church help.

Thursday night potluck supper. Prayer and medication to follow.

The rosebud on the altar this morning is to announce the birth of David Alan Belzer, the sin of Rev. and Mrs Julius Belzer.

This afternoon there will be a meeting in the south and north ends of the church. Children will be baptised at both ends.

Tuesday there will be an ice-cream social at 4 pm. All ladies giving milk please come early.

Thursday at 5 pm there will be a meeting of the Little Mothers Club. All wishing to become Little Mothers, please see the minister in his private study.

This being Easter Sunday, we will ask Mrs Lewis to come forward and lay an egg on the altar.

Next Sunday, a special collection will be taken to defray the cost of the new carpet. All those wishing to do something on the new carpet will come forward and get a piece of paper.

The ladies of the church have cast off clothing of every kind and they may be seen in the church basement Friday.

A bean supper will be held on Tuesday evening in the church basement. Music will follow.

At the early evening service tonight, the sermon topic will be 'What is Hell?' Come early and listen to our choir practise.

Weight Watchers will meet at 7 pm at the Presbyterian Church. Please use large double door at the side entrance.

Pastor is on vacation. Massages can be given to the church secretary.

Eight new choir robes are needed, due to the addition of several new members and to the deterioration of some older ones.

Mrs Johnson will be entering the hospital this week for testes.

The Senior Choir invites any member of the congregation who enjoys sinning to join the choir.

Please join us as we show our support for Amy and Alan who are preparing for the girth of their first child.

The Lutheran Men's Group will meet at 6 pm. Steak, mashed potatoes, green beans, bread and dessert will be served for a nominal feel.

〜〜〜〜〜〜

Dijon vu – the same mustard as before.

〜〜〜〜〜〜

Puritanism: the haunting fear that someone, somewhere may be happy.

Points to Ponder

Why do we say something is out of whack? What is a whack?

Do infants enjoy infancy as much as adults enjoy adultery?

If a pig loses its voice, is it disgruntled?

If love is blind, why is lingerie so popular?

Why is the man who invests all your money called a broker?

Why do croutons come in airtight packages? It's just stale bread to begin with.

Why are a wise man and a wise guy opposites?

Why do overlook and oversee mean opposite things?

If horrific means to make horrible, does terrific mean to make terrible?

Why is it that if someone tells you that there are one billion stars in the universe you will believe them, but if they tell you a wall has wet paint you have to touch it to be sure?

A bus station is where a bus stops. A train station is where a train stops. On my desk I have a work station...

Can atheists get insurance for acts of God?

I believe five out of four people have trouble with fractions.

How come you never hear about gruntled employees?

How much faith does it take to be an atheist?

If a tin whistle is made out of tin (and it is), then what exactly is a fog horn made out of?

If atheists say there is no God, who pops up the next tissue in the box?

If vegetable oil comes from vegetables, where does baby oil come from?

Do Lipton employees take coffee breaks?

What was the best thing *before* sliced bread?

Reasons Why Alcohol Should Be Served at Work

It's an incentive to show up.

It reduces stress.

It leads to more honest communications.

It reduces complaints about low pay.

It cuts down on time off because you can work with a hangover.

Employees tell management what they think, not what management wants to hear.

It helps save on heating costs in the winter.

It encourages car pooling.

It increases job satisfaction because if you have a bad job, you don't care.

It eliminates holidays because people would rather come to work.

It makes fellow employees look better.

It makes the cafeteria food taste better.

Bosses are more likely to hand out raises when they are wasted.

Salary negotiations are a lot more profitable.

Suddenly, burping during a meeting isn't so embarrassing.

Employees work later since there's no longer a need to relax at the bar.

It makes everyone more open with their ideas.

Everyone agrees the work is of better quality after they've had a couple of drinks.

Eliminates the need for employees to get drunk on their lunch break.

It increases the chance of seeing your boss naked.

The cleaner's closet will finally have a use.

Employees will no longer need coffee to sober up.

Sitting on the photocopier will no longer be seen as gross.

Babbling and mumbling incoherently will be common language.

Actual Label Instructions on Consumer Goods

On a hair dryer: Do not use while sleeping.

On a bag of crisps: You could be a winner! No purchase necessary. Details inside.

On a bar of soap: Directions – use like regular soap.

On frozen dinners: Serving suggestion – defrost.

On a hotel-provided shower cap in a box: Fits one head.

On a tiramisu dessert: Do not turn upside down. (Printed on the bottom of the box.)

On a bread pudding: Product will be hot after heating.

On packaging for an iron: Do not iron clothes on body.

On children's cough medicine: Do not drive car or operate machinery.

On sleeping tablets: Warning – may cause drowsiness.

On a kitchen knife: Warning – keep out of children.

On a string of Christmas lights: For indoor or outdoor use only.

On a pack of peanuts: Warning – contains nuts.

On an airline's packet of nuts: Instructions – open packet, eat nuts.

On a chainsaw: Do not attempt to stop chain with your hands.

How to Keep a Healthy Level of Insanity in the Workplace

Page yourself over the intercom. (Don't disguise your voice.)

Make up nicknames for all your co-workers and refer to them only by these names. 'That's a good point, Sparky. No I'm sorry I'm going to have to disagree with you there, Chachi.'

Put up mosquito netting around your cubicle.

Arrive at a meeting late, say you're sorry, but you didn't have time for lunch, and you're going to be nibbling during the meeting. During the meeting eat five entire raw potatoes.

Insist that your e-mail address be zena_goddess_of_fire@companyname.com

Every time someone asks you to do something, ask them if they want fries with that.

Encourage your colleagues to join you in a little synchronised chair dancing.

Put your garbage can on your desk. Label it 'in'.

Determine how many cups of coffee is 'too many'.

Develop an unnatural fear of staplers.

For a relaxing break, get away from it all with a mask and snorkel in the fish tank. If no one notices, take out your snorkel and see how many you can catch in your mouth.

Put decaf in the coffeemaker for three weeks. Once everyone has got over their caffeine addictions, switch to espresso.

~~~~~~

The sex was so good that even the neighbours had a cigarette.

Some Time-honoured Truths

Don't sweat the petty things, and don't pet the sweaty things.

One tequila, two tequila, three tequila, floor.

One nice thing about egotists: they don't talk about other people.

To be intoxicated is to feel sophisticated but not be able to say it.

The older you get, the better you realise you were.

I doubt, therefore I might be.

Age is a very high price to pay for maturity.

Procrastination is the art of keeping up with yesterday.

A fool and his money are soon partying.

Before they invented drawing boards, what did they go back to?

If one synchronised swimmer drowns, do the rest have to drown too?

If work is so terrific, how come they have to pay you to do it?

If you're born again, do you have two belly buttons?

If you ate pasta and antipasta, would you still be hungry?

Funny Signs

At a restaurant: Tip-ing is not a city in China.

Seen on an electrical appliance store: Go modern! Go gas! Go BOOM!

Emergency evacuation plan posted in various places around an office building: Run like hell!

At a septic tank service: Call Monday thru Friday, sorry, we haul milk on weekends.

Sporting goods store: With fishing season upon us we have plenty of crappie poles to fill your needs.

Billboard sign on a highway: Nobody reads billboards... but you just did.

In an airline office in Copenhagen: We take your bags and send them in all directions.

In a hotel in Acapulco: The manager has personally passed all the water served here.

On the door of a Moscow hotel room: If this is your first visit to the USSR, you are welcome to it.

In a Bangkok dry cleaners: Drop your trousers here for best results.

In a hotel in Zurich: Because of the impropriety of entertaining guests of the opposite sex in the bedroom, it is suggested that the lobby be used for this purpose.

On a dock: Safety ladder, climb at own risk.

In a doctor's office in Rome: Specialist in women and other diseases.

In a Bangkok temple: It is forbidden to enter a woman even a foreigner if dressed as a man.

On the taps in men's toilets in Finland: To stop the drip, turn cock to right.

On the menu in a Swiss restaurant: Our wines leave you nothing to hope for.

In a laundry in Rome: Ladies, leave your clothes here and spend the afternoon having a good time.

In the window of a furrier's shop in Sweden: Fur coats made for ladies from their own skin.

At a zoo in Budapest: Please do not feed the animals. If you have any suitable food, give it to the guard on duty.

Woman's Instruction Booklet

Never do housework. No man ever made love to a woman because the house was spotless.

Remember you are known by the idiot you accompany.

Don't imagine you can change a man – unless he's in nappies.

So many men – so many reasons not to sleep with any of them.

If they put a man on the moon, they should be able to put them all there.

Tell him you're not his type – you have a pulse.

Never let your man's mind wander. It's too little to be let out alone.

The only reason men are on this planet is that vibrators can't dance or buy drinks.

Never sleep with a man who's named his penis.

Go for younger men. You might as well. They never mature anyway.

A man who can dress himself without looking like Forrest Gump is unquestionably gay.

Definition of a bachelor: a man who has missed the opportunity to make some woman miserable.

Women don't make fools of men. Most of them are the do-it-yourself types.

The best way to get a man to do something is to suggest they are too old for it.

Love is blind, but marriage is a real eye-opener.

If you want a committed man, look in a mental hospital.

If he asks what sort of books you're interested in, tell him cheque books.

A man's idea of serious commitment is usually 'Oh all right, I'll stay the night.'

Women sleep with men, who if they were women, they wouldn't even bother to have lunch with.

Remember a sense of humour does not mean that you tell him jokes, it means you laugh at his.

If he asks you if you're faking it tell him no, you're just practising.

Sadly, all men are created equal.

When he asks you if he's your first, tell him 'you may be, you look familiar.'

Women don't blink during foreplay because they don't have time.

It take one million sperm to fertilise one egg because they won't stop to ask directions.

Men and sperm are similar as they both have a one-in-a-million chance of becoming a human being.

A man shows that he is planning for the future by buying two cases of beer.

Men and government bonds are different as the bonds mature.

Blonde jokes are short so men can remember them.

It is difficult to find men who are sensitive, caring and good looking as they all already have boyfriends.

A woman who knows where her husband is every night is a widow.

After creating man God said 'I must be able to do better than that.'

Men and parking spots are alike as good ones are always taken and the free ones are mostly handicapped or extremely small.

How to Impress a Woman

Compliment her, cuddle her, kiss her, caress her, love her, stroke her, comfort her, protect her, hold her, spend money on her, wine and dine her, buy things for her, listen to her, care for her, stand by her, support her, go to the ends of the earth for her.

How to Impress a Man

Show up naked, with beer.

Various Philosophies Explained in Terms of Two Cows

Socialism – You have two cows. You keep one and give one to your neighbour.

Communism – You have two cows. The government takes them both and provides you with milk.

Fascism – You have two cows. The government takes them both and sells you the milk.

Nazism – You have two cows. The government takes them both and shoots you.

Bureaucracy – You have two cows. The government takes them both, shoots one, milks the other, pays you for the milk, then pours it down the drain.

Capitalism – You have two cows. You sell one and buy a bull.

Surrealism – You have two giraffes. The government requires you to take harmonica lessons.

Advertising at its Best

2 female Boston terrier puppies, 7 weeks old, perfect markings, 555-1234. Leave mess.

Lost: small apricot poodle. Reward. Neutered. Like one of the family.

A superb and inexpensive restaurant. Fine food expertly served by waitresses in appetising forms.

Dinner special – turkey $2.35; chicken or beef $2.25; children $2.00.

For sale: an antique desk suitable for lady with thick legs and large drawers.

Four-poster bed, 101 years old. Perfect for antique lover.

Now is your chance to have your ears pierced and get an extra pair to take home, too.

Wanted: 50 girls for stripping machine operators in factory.

Wanted: Unmarried girls to pick fresh fruit and produce at night.

We do not tear your clothing with machinery. We do it carefully by hand.

For sale: three canaries of undermined sex.

For sale: eight puppies from a German Shepherd and an Alaskan hussy.

Great dames for sale.

Have several very old dresses from grandmother in beautiful condition.

Tired of cleaning yourself? Let me do it.

Dog for sale: eats anything and is fond of children.

Holiday special: have your home exterminated.

Mt Kilimanjaro, the breathtaking backdrop for the Serena Lodge. Swim in the lovely pool while you drink it all in.

Get rid of aunts: Zap does the job in 24 hours.

Toaster: A gift that every member of the family appreciates. Automatically burns toast.

Sheer stockings. Designed for fancy dress, but so serviceable that lots of women wear nothing else.

Stock up and save. Limit: one.

For rent: 6-room hated apartment.

Man, honest. Will take anything.

Wanted: chambermaid in rectory. Love in, $200 a month. References required.

Man wanted to work in dynamite factory. Must be willing to travel.

Used cars: Why go elsewhere to be cheated? Come here first!

Christmas sale. Handmade gifts for the hard-to-find person.

Wanted: Haircutter. Excellent growth potential.

Wanted: Man to take care of cow that does not smoke or drink.

3-year-old teacher needed for pre-school. Experience preferred.

Our experienced Mum will care of your child. Fenced yard, meals, and smacks included.

Our bikinis are exciting. They are simply the tops.

Auto repair service. Free pick-up and delivery. Try us once, you'll never go anywhere again.

Illiterate? Write today for free help.

Girl wanted to assist magician in cutting-off-head illusion. Blue Cross and salary.

Wanted: Widower with school-age children requires person to assume general housekeeping duties. Must be capable of contributing to growth of family.

And now, the Superstore – unequalled in size, unmatched in variety, unrivalled inconvenience.

We will oil your sewing machine and adjust tension in your home for $1.00.

He who laughs last thinks the slowest.

A torch is a case for holding dead batteries.

Maintenance Complaints

Here are some actual complaints submitted recently by pilots to maintenance engineers pertaining to problems that are to be fixed prior to the aircraft's next flight. After attending to the complaints, the maintenance crews are required to log the details of the action taken to fix these complaints.

(P) = The problem logged by the pilot
(S) = The solution and the action taken by maintenance engineers

(P) Left inside main tyre almost needs replacement.
(S) Almost replaced left inside main tyre.

(P) Test flight okay, except autoland very rough.
(S) Autoland not installed on this aircraft.

(P) Number 2 propeller seeping prop fluid.
(S) Number 2 propeller seepage normal. Number 1, 3 and 4 propellers lack normal seepage.

(P) Something loose in cockpit.
(S) Something tightened in cockpit.

(P) Evidence of leak on right main landing gear.
(S) Evidence removed.

(P) DME volume unbelievably loud.
(S) Volume set to more believable level.

(P) Dead bugs on windshield.
(S) Live bugs on backorder.

(P) Autopilot in altitude hold mode produces a 200 fpm descent.
(S) Cannot reproduce problem on ground.

(P) IFF inoperative.
(S) IFF always inoperative in off mode.

(P) Friction locks cause throttle levers to stick.
(S) That's what they're there for!

(P) Number three engine missing.
(S) Engine found on right wing after brief search.

(P) Aircraft handles funny.
(S) Aircraft warned to straighten up, 'fly right' and be serious!

(P) Target radar hums.
(S) Reprogrammed target radar with the words.

~~~~~~~~~

I used to have a handle on life. Then it broke.

~~~~~~~~~

I'd give my right arm to be ambidextrous.

~~~~~~~~~

I believe in youthenasia.

Men's Guide to Women's English

When Women Say — They Really Mean

When Women Say	They Really Mean
'We need...'	I want...
'It's your decision.'	The correct decision should be obvious by now.
'Do what you want.'	You'll pay for this later.
'We need to talk.'	I need to complain.
'Sure... go ahead.'	Don't.
'I'm not upset.'	Of course I'm upset, you moron!
'You're certainly attentive tonight.'	Is sex all you think about?
'I'm not emotional! And I'm not overreacting!'	I've got my period.
'Be romantic, turn out the lights.'	I have flabby thighs.
'This kitchen is so inconvenient.'	I want a new house.
'I heard a noise.'	I noticed you were almost asleep.'

'Do you love me?' — I'm going to ask for something expensive.

'How much do you love me?' — I did something today you're really not going to like.

'Is my bum fat?' — Tell me I'm beautiful.

'You have to learn to communicate.' — Just agree with me.

'Yes.' — No.

'No.' — No.

'Maybe.' — No.

'I'm sorry.' — You'll be sorry.

'Do you like this recipe?' — It's easy, so you'd better get used to it.

'Was that the baby?' — Why don't you get out of bed and walk him until he goes to sleep?

'Can't we just be friends?' — There is no way in hell I am going to let any part of your body touch any part of mine again.

'I just need some space.' — I just need some space without you in it.

'Do I look fat in this dress?' We haven't had a fight in a while.

'No, pizza's fine.' Cheap git.

'I just do not want a boyfriend.' I just do not want (you as) a boyfriend.

'Oh, no, I will pay for myself.' I'm just pretending to be nice, there is no way I am going Dutch.

'Oh yes! Right there.' Well, near there. I just want to get this over with.

'I'm just going out with the girls.' We are gonna get sloppy and make fun of you and your friends.

'There's no one else.' I am sleeping with your best friend.

'Size doesn't count.' Size doesn't count unless I want an orgasm.

Women's Guide to Men's English

What Men Say

They Really Mean

Hello. Let's cut the talk and go have sex.

'How are you?'   How are you in bed, I
                                       mean.

'I'd like a discreet   I want sex, but
relationship.'   I'm married.

'I'll be out of town for a   I'll be spending
few days.'   time with the wife.

'I'm a novelist.'   I have 10 unpublished
                                       books.

'I'm coming out of a long   My wife is
relationship.'   divorcing me.

'I'm consulting.'   I'm looking for a job.

'I'm divorced.'   I just slipped off my
                                       wedding ring.

'I'm in television.'   I fix them.

'I'm involved in banking.'   I'm a bank guard.

'I'm self-employed.'   I just got fired.

'I'm sorry I flirted with your   I'm sorry I got
sister.'   caught.

'I'm thinking of relocating.'   I can't find a job locally
                                       in this town.

'I can't leave my wife   Be patient forever.
just yet.'

'I enjoy reading.'	That's right – *Playboy* and *Penthouse*.
'I have the Midas touch.	I install mufflers.
'I like a woman who is intelligent.'	As long as she thinks I'm smarter.
'I love opera.'	I want sex, but I've seen an opera once.
'I work high up in an executive office.'	I'm a window washer.
'I work with computers.'	I'm a cashier at a petrol station.
'I'm looking for a satisfying relationship.'	I want sex.
'My business is really hot right now!'	I hand out towels in a steam room.
'My job keeps me running.'	I'm a messenger.
'My wife and I are separated.'	She's at home and I'm here at the bar.
'I'm hungry.'	I'm hungry.
'I'm sleepy.'	I'm sleepy.
'I'm tired.'	I'm tired.
'Do you want to go to a movie?'	I'd eventually like to have sex with you.

'Can I take you out to dinner?'	I'd eventually like to have sex with you.
'Can I call you sometime?'	I'd eventually like to have sex with you.
'May I have this dance?'	I'd eventually like to have sex with you.
'Nice dress!'	Nice cleavage!
'You look tense, let me give you a massage.'	I want to fondle you.
'What's wrong?'	I guess sex tonight is out of the question.
'I'm bored.'	Do you want to have sex?
'I love you.'	Let's have sex now.
'Let's talk.'	I am trying to impress you by showing that I am a very deep person and maybe then you'd agree to have sex with me.
'Will you marry me?'	I want to make it illegal for you to have sex with any other guys.

'I like that one better.'
(while shopping)

Pick any bloody dress and let's go home!

'I need you.'

My hand is tired.

'How do I compare with your other boyfriends?'

Is my penis really that small?

'It is just orange juice, try it.'

Three more shots, and she'll have her legs around my head.

'I want you back.'

I want to boink you tonight.

'We've been through so much together.'

If it weren't for you, I never would have lost my virginity.

'I miss you so much.'

I am so horny that my roommate is starting to look good.

'I'm going fishing.'

I'm going to drink myself dangerously stupid, and stand by a stream with a stick in my hand, while the fish swim by in complete safety.

'It would take too long to explain.'

I have no idea how it works.

'It's a guy thing.' There is no rational thought pattern connected with it, and you have no chance at all of making it logical.

'What's wrong?'	What meaningless self-inflicted psychological trauma are you going through now?
'Can I help with dinner?'	Why isn't it already on the table?
'Uh huh', 'sure, honey' or 'yes, dear'	Absolutely nothing. It's a conditioned response.
'We're going to be late.'	Now I have a legitimate excuse to drive like a maniac.
'I was listening to you. It's just that I have other things on my mind.'	I was wondering if that redhead over there is wearing a bra.
'Take a break, honey, you're working too hard.'	I can't hear the game over the vacuum cleaner.
'That's interesting, dear.'	Are you still talking?

'It's a really good movie.'

It's got guns, knives, fast cars and beautiful naked women.

'That's women's work.'

It's difficult, dirty, and thankless.

'You know how bad my memory is.'

I remember the theme song to 'F Troop', the address of the first girl I ever kissed and the vehicle identification and license plates of every car I've ever owned, but I forgot your birthday.

'I was just thinking about you, and got you these roses.'

The girl selling them on the corner was a babe.

'Oh, don't fuss. I just cut myself, it's no big deal.'

I have actually severed a limb, but will bleed to death before I admit I'm hurt.

'Hey, I've got my reasons for what I'm doing.'

And I hope I think of some pretty soon.

'I can't find it.'

It didn't fall into my outstretched hands, so I'm completely clueless.

'What did I do this time?' What did you catch me at?

'I heard you.' I haven't the foggiest clue what you just said, and am hoping desperately that I can fake it well enough so that you don't spend the next three days yelling at me.

'You know I could never love anyone else.' I am used to the way you yell at me, and realise it could be worse.

'You look terrific.' Oh, God, please don't try on one more outfit. I'm starving.

'I'm not lost. I know exactly where we are.' No one will ever see us alive again.

'We share the housework.' I make the messes, she cleans them up.

~~~~~~

*How do they get kangaroos
to cross at that yellow sign?*

Sex-related Truths

Nothing improves with age.

Sex has no calories.

Sex takes up the least amount of time and causes the most amount of trouble.

Sex is like snow; you never know how many inches you are going to get or how long it is going to last.

Virginity can be cured.

Never sleep with anyone crazier than yourself.

You shouldn't rub the lamp if you don't want the genie to come out.

Sex is dirty only if it's done right.

It is always the wrong time of month.

When the lights are out, all women are beautiful.

Sex is hereditary. If your parents never had it, chances are you won't either.

Sow your wild oats on Saturday night – then on Sunday pray for crop failure.

It was not the apple on the tree but the pair on the ground that caused the trouble in the garden.

You shouldn't fake it because men would rather be ineffective than deceived.

Sex discriminates against the shy and the ugly.

Love your neighbour, but don't get caught.

One good turn gets most of the blankets.

You cannot produce a baby in one month by impregnating nine women.

Love is the triumph of imagination over intelligence.

Never lie down with a woman who's got more troubles than you.

Abstain from wine, women and song; mostly song.

Never argue with a women when she's tired – or rested.

It is better to be looked over than overlooked.

A man can be happy with any woman as long as he doesn't love her.

There is no difference between a wise man and a fool when they fall in love.

Never say no.

~~~~~~~~

The early bird may get the worm, but it's the second mouse that gets the cheese.

Final University Exam

Instructions: Read each question carefully.
You have two hours to answer all questions.
Begin immediately.

History: Describe the history of the papacy from its origins through to the present day, concentrating especially, but not exclusively, on its social, political, economic, religious and philosophical impact on Europe, Asia, America and Africa. Be brief, concise and specific.

Medicine: You have been provided with a razor blade, a piece of gauze, and a bottle of scotch whisky. Remove your appendix. Do not suture until your work has been inspected.

Public Speaking: 2500 riot-crazed Aborigines are storming the classroom. Calm them. You may use any ancient language except Latin or Greek.

Biology: Create life. Estimate the differences in subsequent human culture if this form of life had developed 500 million years earlier, with special attention to its probable effect on the English parliamentary system. Prove your thesis.

Music: Write a piano concerto. Orchestrate and perform it with flute and drum. You will find a piano under your seat.

Psychology: Based on your knowledge of their works, evaluate the emotional stability, degree of adjustment, and repressed frustration of each of the following: Alexander of Aphrodisis, Rameses II, Hammuarabi. Support your evaluation with quotations from each man's work, making appropriate references. It is not necessary to translate.

Sociology: Estimate the sociological problems which might accompany the end of the world. Construct an experiment to test your theory.

Engineering: The disassembled parts of a high-powered rifle have been placed on your desk. You will also find an instruction manual, printed in Swahili. In 10 minutes, a hungry Bengal tiger will be admitted to the room. Take whatever action you feel necessary. Be prepared to justify your decision.

Physics: Explain the nature of matter. Include in your answer an evaluation of the impact of the development of mathematics on science.

Philosophy: Sketch the development of human thought. Estimate its significance. Compare with the development of any other kind of thought.

General Knowledge: Describe in detail. Be objective and specific.

Things Never to Say During Sex

What is *that*?

Is it in?

You're kidding, right?

(Phone rings.) Hello? Oh nothing, and you?

Do I have to pay for this?

You look better in the dark.

You have the same bra my mum does (worse if the girl says it).

I hope you don't expect a raise for this...

Did I tell you I have herpes?

Now we must get married.

Are you trying to be funny?

Is that smell coming from you?

Haven't you ever done this before?

Do you know what some female spiders do after sex?

But you just started!

Don't touch that!

I think my dad is listening at the door.

Smile for the camera, honey!

Get your hand out of there!

I knew you wore a padded bra!

Hold on, let me change the channel...

Stop moaning, you sound so stupid.

I'm sorry, I wasn't listening.

It's okay honey, I can imagine that it's bigger.

God I wish you were a real woman.

By the way, when I drove over here, I ran over your dog...

Oh Susan, Susan... I mean Donna... shit.

Is it okay if after this I never see you again?

Did I forget to tell you I got worms from my cat?

Don't make that face at me!

How come we each have a penis?

Of course you can't be on top, you're too fat, you'll kill me!

No problem, we'll try again later when you can satisfy me too.

Get off me, I'll do it myself!

The only reason I'm doing this is because I'm drunk.

My mum taught me this...

Should I ask why you're bleeding?

This is my pet rat, Larry....

I haven't had this much sex since I was a hooker!

Don't squirm, you'll spill my beer.

Did I tell you where my cold sore came from?

Fun Things to do While Driving

At stop lights, eye the person in the next car suspiciously. With a look of fear, lock your doors.

Stop at the green lights.

Pass cars, then drive very slowly.

Honk frequently without motivation.

Wave at people often. If they wave back, offer an angry look and an obscene gesture.

Let pedestrians know who's boss.

Restart your car at every stop light.

Hang numerous car-fresheners on the rear-view mirror. Talk to them, stroking them lovingly.

Have some passengers in the back who are having wild, noisy sex.

Stop and smell the roses along the way.

Politically Correct Terms

Dirty old man = Sexually focused chronologically gifted individual

Perverted = Sexually dysfunctional

Serial killer = Person with difficult-to-meet needs

Lazy = Motivationally deficient

Fat = Horizontally challenged

Fail = Achieve a deficiency

Dishonest = Ethically disoriented

Clumsy = Uniquely coordinated

Body odour = Nondiscretionary fragrance

Alive = Temporarily metabolically abled

Worst = Least best

Wrong = Differently logical

Ugly = Cosmetically different

Unemployed = Involuntarily leisured

Dead = Living impaired

Vagrant = Non-specifically destinationed individual

Spendthrift = Negative saver

Stoned = Chemically inconvenienced

Pregnant = Parasitically oppressed

Ignorant = Knowledge-based nonpossessor

Dumb and Dumber

The following are questions actually asked of witnesses by attorneys during trials and, in certain cases, the responses given by the insightful witnesses:

Q. What is your date of birth?
A. July fifteenth.
Q. What year?
A. Every year.

Q. What gear were you in at the moment of the impact?
A. Gucci sweats and Reeboks.

Q. How old is your son – the one living with you?
A. Thirty-eight or thirty-five, I can't remember which.
Q. How long has he lived with you?
A. Forty-five years.

Q. What was the first thing your husband said to you when he woke that morning?
A. He said, 'Where am I, Cathy?'
Q. And why did that upset you?
A. My name is Susan.

Q. She had three children, right?
A. Yes.
Q. How many were boys?
A. None.
Q. Were there any girls?

Q. You say the stairs went down to the basement?
A. Yes.
Q. And these stairs, did they go up also?

Q. How was your first marriage terminated?
A. By death.
Q. And by whose death was it terminated?

Q. 'Now doctor, isn't it true that when a person dies in his sleep, he doesn't know about it until the next morning?'

Q. 'Were you present when your picture was taken?'

Q. 'How far apart were the vehicles at the time of the collision?'

Q. 'You were there until the time you left, is that true?'

Q. 'How many times have you committed suicide?'

Q. Doctor, how many autopsies have you performed on dead people?
A. All my autopsies are performed on dead people.

Q. Do you recall the time that you examined the body?
A. The autopsy started around 8:30 pm.

Q. And Mr Descartes was dead at the time?
A. No, he was sitting on the table wondering why I was doing an autopsy.

Q. Doctor, before you performed the autopsy, did you check for a pulse?

A. No.

Q. Did you check for blood pressure?

A. No.

Q. Did you check for breathing?

A. No.

Q. So, then it is possible that the patient was alive when you began the autopsy

A. No.

Q. How can you be so sure, Doctor?

A. Because his brain was sitting on my desk in a jar.

Q. But nevertheless, could the patient have still been alive?

A. It is possible that he could have been alive and practising law somewhere.

~~~~~~~~~

The gene pool could use a little chlorine.

~~~~~~~~~

Where there's a will, I want to be in it.

Crazy Calls

A transcript of the new call centre recently set up for the Acme Mental Health Institute.

Hello and welcome to the Mental Health Hotline.

If you are obsessive-compulsive, press 1 repeatedly.

If you are co-dependent, please ask someone to press 2 for you.

If you have multiple personalities, press 3, 4, 5 and 6.

If you are paranoid, we know who you are and what you want. Stay on the line so we can trace the call.

If you are delusional, press 7 and your call will be transferred to the mothership.

If you are schizophrenic, listen carefully and a small voice will tell you which number to press.

If you are manic-depressive, it doesn't matter which number you press, no one will answer.

If you are dyslexic, press 865325478929136.

If you have a nervous disorder, please fidget with the hash key until a representative comes on the line.

If you have amnesia, press 8 and state your name, address, phone number, date of birth, credit card number and your mother's maiden name.

If you have post-traumatic stress disorder, slowly and carefully press 000.

If you have bi-polar disorder, please leave a message after the beep, or before the beep. Or after the beep.

Please wait for the beep.

If you have short term memory loss, press 9.

If you have short term memory loss, press 9.

If you have short term memory loss, press 9.

If you have low self-esteem, please hang up. All our operators are too busy to talk to you.

Anagrams

An anagram is a word or phrase made by rearranging the letters of another word or phrase. Judging by the following anagrams, someone out there has way too much time on their hands.

Dormitory: Dirty room

Evangelist: Evil's agent

Desperation: A rope ends it

The Morse Code: Here come dots

Slot machines: Cash lost in 'em

Animosity: Is no amity

Mother-in-law: Woman Hitler

Snooze alarms: Alas! No more zs

Semolina: Is no meal

The public art galleries: Large picture halls, I bet

A decimal point: I'm a dot in place

The earthquakes: That queer shake

Eleven plus two: Twelve plus one

Contradiction: Accord not in it

This one's truly amazing: To be or not to be: that is the question, whether tis nobler in the mind to suffer the slings and arrows of outrageous fortune. *The anagram:* In one of the Bard's best-thought-of tragedies, our insistent hero, Hamlet, queries on two fronts about how life turns rotten.

And for the grand finale: That's one small step for man, one giant leap for mankind – Neil Armstrong *The anagram:* Thin man ran; makes a large stride, left planet, pins flag on moon! On to Mars!

~~~~~~

Few women admit their age. Few men act theirs.

~~~~~~

Consciousness: that annoying time between naps.

Answering Machine Messages

'Hi! John's answering machine is broken. This is his refrigerator. Please speak very slowly, and I'll stick your message to myself with one of these magnets.'

'A is for academics, B is for beer. One of those reasons is why we're not here. So leave a message and I'll get back to you.'

'Hi. This is John. If you are the phone company, I already sent the money. If you are my parents, please send money. If you are my financial aid institution, you didn't lend me enough money. If you are my friends, you owe me money. If you are a female, don't worry, I have plenty of money.'

'Hi. Now you say something.'

'Hi, I'm not home right now but my answering machine is, so you can talk to it instead. Wait for the beep.'

'Hello. I am David's answering machine. What are you?'

'Hello, you are talking to a machine. I am capable of receiving messages.'

'This is not an answering machine – this is a telepathic thought-recording device. After the tone, think about your name, your reason for calling and number where I can reach you, and I'll think about returning your call.'

'My owners do not need their walls painted, windows washed, or their carpets steam-cleaned. They give to charity through their office and do not need their picture taken. If you're still with me, leave your name and number and they will get back to you.'

'Hi. I am probably home, I'm just avoiding someone I don't like. Leave me a message, and if I don't call back, it's you.'

'If you are a burglar, then we're probably at home cleaning our weapons right now and can't come to the phone. Otherwise, we probably aren't home and it's safe to leave us a message.'

'Hi, this is George. I'm sorry I can't answer the phone right now. Leave a message, and then wait by your phone until I call you back.'

'Please leave a message. However, you have the right to remain silent. Everything you say will be recorded and will be used by us.'

~~~~~~

Lottery: a tax on people who are bad at maths.

~~~~~~

Artificial intelligence usually beats real stupidity.

Guidance Counsellor

The following information was gained through much arduous research involving men and women from all backgrounds and walks of life. It consists of the most frequently asked questions of women – relationships, sex and life in general. All women who read this are encouraged to use the wisdom contained therein to change their behaviour in accordance with the truths set out below.

Q:How do I know if I'm ready for sex?

A:Ask your boyfriend. He'll know when the time is right. When it comes to love and sex, men are much more responsible, since they're not as emotionally confused as women. It's a proven fact.

Q:Should I have sex on the first date?

A:Yes. Before if possible.

Q:What exactly happens during the act of sex?

A:Again, this is entirely up to the man. Just remember that you must do whatever he tells you without question. He may ask you to do certain things that may at first seem strange to you. Do them anyway.

Q:How long should the sex act last?

A:This is a natural and normal part of nature, so don't feel ashamed or embarrassed. After you've finished making love, he'll have a natural desire to leave you suddenly, go out with his mates to a pool hall or a really sleazy bar and get drunk.

Q: What is afterplay?

A: After a man has finished making love, he needs to replenish his manly energy. Afterplay is simply a list of important activities for you to do after lovemaking. This includes lighting his cigarette, making him a sandwich or pizza, bringing him a few beers, or leaving him alone to sleep while you go out and buy him an expensive gift.

Q: Does the size of the penis matter?

A: Yes. Although many women believe that quality, not quantity, is important, studies show this is simply not true. The average erect male penis measures about three inches. Anything longer than that is extremely rare and if by some chance your lover's sexual organ is four inches or over, you should go down on your knees and thank your lucky stars and do everything possible to please him, such as doing his laundry, cleaning his apartment and/or buying him an expensive gift.

Q: What about the female orgasm?

A: What about it? There's no such thing. It's a myth.

It's the Size That Counts....

I've smoked fatter joints than that.

Who circumcised you?

Why don't we just cuddle?

You know they have surgery to fix that.

It's more fun to look at.

Make it dance.

You know, there's a tower in Italy like that.

My last boyfriend was four inches bigger.

It's okay, we'll work around it.

Will it squeak if I squeeze it?

Can I be honest with you?

My eight-year-old brother has one like that.

How sweet, you brought incense.

This explains your car.

You must be a growing boy.

Maybe if we water it, it'll grow.

Have you ever thought of working in a sideshow?

All right, a treasure hunt!

I didn't know they came that small.

Why is God punishing you?

I never saw one like that before.

What do you call this?

But it still works, right?

I hear excessive masturbation shrinks it.

Maybe it looks better in natural light.

Why don't we skip right to the cigarettes?

Oh, I didn't know you were in an accident.

Aww, it's hiding.

Are you cold?

If you get me real drunk first.

Is that an optical illusion?

What is that?

Does it come with an air pump?

So this is why you're supposed to judge people on personality.

~~~~~~~~

Does fuzzy logic tickle?

~~~~~~~~

'Very funny, Scotty. Now beam me down my clothes.'

The Rules of Bedroom Golf

Each player shall furnish his own equipment for play. Play on a course must be approved by the owner of the hole. Unlike outdoor golf, the object is to get the club in the hole and keep the balls out.

For most effective play, the club should have a firm shaft. Course owners are permitted to check shaft stiffness before play begins. Course owners reserve the right to restrict club length to avoid damage to the hole.

The object of the game is to take as many strokes as necessary until the course owner is satisfied that play is completed. Failure to do so may result in being denied permission to play the course again.

It is considered bad form to begin playing the hole immediately upon arrival at the course. The experienced player will normally take time to admire the entire course with special attention to well-formed bunkers.

Players are cautioned not to mention other courses they have played, or are currently playing, to the owner of the course being played. Upset course owners have been known to damage players equipment for this reason.

Players are encouraged to bring proper rain gear for their own protection.

Players should ensure themselves that their match has been properly scheduled, particularly when a new course is being played for the first time. Previous players have been known to become irate if they discover someone else playing on what they considered to be a private course.

Players should not assume a course is in shape for play at all times. Some players may be embarrassed if they find the course to be temporarily under repair.

Players are advised to be extremely tactful in this situation. More advanced players will find alternative means of play when this is the case.

The course owner is responsible for manicuring and pruning any bush around the hole to allow for improved viewing of alignment with, and approach to the hole.

Slow play is encouraged. However, players should be prepared to proceed at a quicker pace, at least temporarily, at the course owner's request.

It is considered outstanding performance, time permitting, to play the same hole several times in one match.

~~~~~~~~

I wouldn't be caught dead with a necrophiliac.

The Best and Worst Country and Western Song Titles

Get Your Biscuits in the Oven and Your Buns in Bed

Get Your Tongue Outta My Mouth 'Cause I'm Kissing You Goodbye

Her Teeth Were Stained, But Her Heart Was Pure

How Can I Miss You if You Won't Go Away?

I Can't Get Over You, So Why Don't You Get Under Me?

I Don't Know Whether to Kill Myself or Go Bowling

I Just Bought a Car From a Guy That Stole My Girl, But The Car Don't Run So I Figure We Got an Even Deal

I Keep Forgettin' I Forgot About You

I Liked You Better Before I Knew You So Well

I Still Miss You Baby, But My Aim's Gettin' Better

I Wouldn't Take Her to a Dog Fight, Cause I'm Afraid She'd Win

I'll Marry You Tomorrow But Let's Honeymoon Tonight

I'm So Miserable Without You, It's Like Having You Here

I've Got Tears in My Ears From Lying On My Back While I Cry Over You

If I Had Shot You When I Wanted To, I'd Be Out By Now

Mama Get a Hammer (There's a Fly on Papa's Head)

My Head Hurts, My Feet Stink, and I Don't Love Jesus

My Wife Ran Off With My Best Friend, and I Sure Do Miss Him

She Got the Ring and I Got the Finger

You Done Tore Out My Heart, and Stomped That Sucker Flat

You're the Reason Our Kids Are So Ugly

Ways to Annoy People

Leave the photocopier set to reduce 200%, extra dark, A3 paper, 99 copies.

Specify that your drive-through order is 'to take away'.

If you have a glass eye, tap on it occasionally with your pen while talking to others.

Insist on keeping your windscreen wipers running in all weather conditions 'to keep them tuned up'.

Reply to everything someone says with 'that's what *you* think'.

Practise making fax and modem noises.

Highlight irrelevant information in scientific papers and 'cc' them to your boss.

Make beeping noises when a large person backs up.

Finish all your sentences with the words 'in accordance with the prophesy'.

Signal that a conversation is over by clamping your hands over your ears.

Adjust the tint on your TV so that all the people are green, and insist to others that you 'like it that way'.

Staple papers in the middle of the page.

Publicly investigate just how slowly you can make a 'croaking' noise.

Decline to be seated at a restaurant, and simply eat their complimentary mints by the cash register.

Buy a large quantity of orange traffic cones and re-route whole streets.

Repeat the following conversation a dozen times: 'Do you hear that?' 'What?' 'It's okay, it's gone now.'

Try playing the William Tell Overture by tapping on the bottom of your chin. When nearly done, announce, 'No, wait, I messed it up' and repeat.

Ask people what gender they are.

type only in lower case.

While making presentations, occasionally bob your head like a parakeet.

Sit in your front yard pointing a hairdryer at passing cars to see if they slow down...

Sing along at the opera.

TYPE ONLY IN UPPER CASE.

More Bad Pick-up Lines

'That dress would look great on the floor next to my bed.'

'Do you want to see something swell?'

'Say, did we go to different schools together?'

'Why don't you come over here, sit on my lap and we'll talk about the first thing that pops up?'

Hand out cards that say: 'Smile if you want to sleep with me.' Watch them try to hold back their laugh.

At the office photocopier: 'Reproducing eh? Can I help? Would you like gin and platonic or do you prefer scotch and sofa?'

'Bond. James Bond.'

'If I told you that you had a great body, would you hold it against me?'

'Wanna play carnival? You sit on my face and I guess how much you weigh.'

'My face is leaving in 10 minutes. Be on it.'

'I'm Irish. Do you have any Irish in you? Would you like some?'

'Do I know you from somewhere, because I don't recognise you with your clothes on?'

'Do you know the essential difference between sex and conversation? (No?) Do you wanna go upstairs and talk?'

More Funny Signs

Sign on an electrician's truck: Let us remove your shorts.

Sign outside a radiator repair shop: Best place in town to take a leak.

Maternity clothes shop: We are open on labour day.

Non-smoking area: If we see you smoking we will assume you are on fire and take appropriate action.

On maternity room door: 'Push, push, push'.

On a front door: Everyone on the premises is a vegetarian except the dog.

Optometrist's office: If you don't see what you're looking for, you've come to the right place.

Scientist's door: Gone fission.

Taxidermist window: We really know our stuff.

Podiatrist's window: Time wounds all heels.

Butcher's window: Let me meat your needs.

Used-car lot: Second-hand cars in first crash condition.

Sign on fence: Salesmen welcome. Dog food is expensive.

Car dealership: The best way to get back on your feet: miss a car payment.

Muffler shop: No appointment necessary. We'll hear you coming.

Hotel: Help! We need inn-experienced people.

Butcher's window: Pleased to meat you.

Dry cleaner's: Drop your pants here.

Beauty shop: Dye now!

Veterinarian's waiting room: Be back in 5 minutes. Sit! Stay!

Music teacher's door: Out Chopin.

At the electric company: We would be delighted if you send in your bill. However, if you don't, you will be.

Computer store: Out for a quick byte.

Bowling alley: Please be quiet. We need to hear a pin drop.

Music library: Bach in a minuet.

Sign in a laundromat: Automatic washing machines: please remove all your clothes when the light goes out.

Sign in a London department store: Bargain basement upstairs.

In an office: Would the person who took the step ladder yesterday please bring it back or further steps will be taken.

Outside a farm: Horse manure 50 cents per pre-packed bag. 20 cents do-it-yourself.

In an office: After tea-break staff should empty the teapot and stand upside down on the draining board.

English sign in a German cafe: Mothers, please wash your hands before eating.

Outside a second-hand shop: We exchange anything – bicycles, lawn mowers, washing machines etc. Why not bring your wife along and get a wonderful bargain?

Sign outside a new town hall which was to be opened by the Prince of Wales: The town hall is closed until opening. It will remain closed after being opened. Open tomorrow.

Outside a photographer's studio: Out to lunch. If not back by five, out for dinner also.

Outside a disco: Smarts is the most exclusive disco in town. Everyone welcome.

Sign warning of quicksand: Quicksand. Any person passing this point will be drowned. By order of the district council.

Notice in a dry cleaner's window: Anyone leaving their garments here for more than 30 days will be disposed of.

Sign on motorway garage: Please do not smoke near our petrol pumps. Your life may not be worth much but our petrol is.

Notice in health food shop window: Closed due to illness.

Sign on a repair shop door: We can repair anything. (Please knock hard on the door – the bell doesn't work.)

Spotted in a safari park: Elephants please stay in your car.

Spotted in a toilet in a London office block: Toilet out of order. Please use floor below.

Dumb Inventions

Solar-powered flashlight

Inflatable dart board

Sliding doors on a submarine

Reusable condoms

Dehydrated water

Pet rocks

Plastic firewood

Soleless shoes

A book on how to read

A flammable fire extinguisher

A glass cricket bat

Wooden soap

Plasticine wire cutters

A water-proof tea bag

A glass hammer

Revolving basement restaurant

Marriage

A successful man is one who makes more money than his wife can spend. A successful woman is one who can find such a man.

Marriage is a three-ring circus: engagement ring, wedding ring, suffering.

My girlfriend told me I should be more affectionate. So I got two girlfriends.

A man meets a genie. The genie tells him he can have whatever he wants provided that his mother-in-law gets double. The man thinks for a moment and then says, 'Okay, give me a million dollars and beat me half to death.'

Men who have pierced ears are better prepared for marriage. They've experienced pain and bought jewellery.

How do most men define marriage? A very expensive way to get your laundry done free.

A little boy asked his father, 'Daddy, how much does it cost to get married?' And the father replied, 'I don't know, son, I'm still paying for it.'

A man said his credit card was stolen but he decided not to report it because the thief was spending less than his wife did.

Love is blind but marriage is an eye-opener.

The most effective way to remember your wife's birthday is to forget it once.

When a man opens the door of his car for his wife, you can be sure of one thing: either the car is new or the wife is new.

Words to live by: do not argue with a spouse who is packing your parachute.

Most Common Rejection Lines...and What They Actually Mean

By Women

I think of you as a brother...
You get on my nerves and are always bugging me.

There's a slight difference in our ages.
You are one Jurassic geezer who looked a lot younger in the nightclub.

I'm not attracted to you in 'that' way.
You are the ugliest dork I've ever laid eyes on.

My life is too complicated right now.
I don't want you spending the whole night or else you may hear phone calls from all the other guys I'm seeing.

I've already got a boyfriend.
(Who's really my male cat and a cheap cask of wine.)

I don't date men where I work.
I wouldn't even date you if you were in the same solar system, let alone building.

It's not you, it's me.
It's not me, it's you.

I'm concentrating on my career.
Even something as boring and unfulfilling as my job is better than a jerk like you.

By Men

I think of you as a sister.
You're ugly.

There's a slight difference in our ages.
You're ugly.

I'm not attracted to you in 'that' way.
You're ugly.

My life is too complicated right now.
You're ugly.

I've got a girlfriend.
You're ugly.

I don't date women where I work.
You're ugly.

It's not you, it's me...
You're ugly.

I'm concentrating on my career.
You're ugly.

I'm celibate.
You're ugly.

Special One-liners

Well this day was a total waste of make-up.

A hard-on doesn't count as personal growth.

Do I look like a f***ing people person?

I started out with nothing and still have most of it left.

You! Off my planet!

If I want to hear the pitter patter of tiny feet, I'll put shoes on my cat.

The bible was written by the same people who said the earth was flat.

Did the aliens forget to remove your anal probe?

Sarcasm is just one more service we offer.

Whatever kind of look you were going for, you missed.

Suburbia: where they tear out all the trees and then name the streets after them.

I'm not your type. I'm not inflatable.

Can I trade this job for whatever's behind door number 2?

Nice perfume. Must you marinate in it?

Too many freaks, not enough circuses.

I thought I wanted a career. Turns out I just wanted pay cheques.

How do I set the laser printer to stun?

It isn't the size, it's the... no, it's the size.

Children's Books You Will Never See

You Are Different and That's Bad

Dad's New Wife Timothy

Pop! Goes The Kitten... and Other Great Microwave Games

Testing Homemade Parachutes Using Only Your Household Pets

The Hardy Boys, the Barbie Twins, and the Vice Squad

Babar Meets the Taxidermist

Curious George and the High-voltage Fence

The Boy Who Died from Eating All His Vegetables

Spend up Big With the Change From Your Mum's Purse

The Pop-up Book of Human Anatomy

Things Rich Kids Have, But You Never Will

Controlling the Playground: Respect through Fear

You Were an Accident

Strangers Have the Best Lollies

The Little Sissy Who Snitched

Some Kittens Can Fly!

Kathy Was So Bad Her Mum Stopped Loving Her

All Dogs Go to Hell

The Kids' Guide to Hitchhiking

When Mummy and Daddy Don't Know the Answer, They Say God Did It

Garfield Gets Feline Leukemia

What Is That Dog Doing to That Other Dog?

Why Can't Mr Fork and Ms Electrical Outlet Be Friends?

Boyle's Law in Regards to Hell

This was an actual question given on a university chemistry exam:

'Is Hell exothermic (gives off heat) or endothermic (absorbs heat)? Support your answer with proof.'

Most of the students wrote proofs of their beliefs using Boyle's Law (gas cools off when it expands and heats up when it is compressed) or some variant. One student, however, wrote the following:

'First, we need to know how the mass of Hell is changing in time. So, we need to know the rate that souls are moving into Hell and the rate they are leaving. I think that we can safely assume that once a soul gets to Hell, it will not leave. Therefore, no souls are leaving.

As for how many souls are entering Hell, let's look at the different religions that exist in the world today. Some of these religions state that if you are not a member of their religion, you will go to Hell. Since there are more than one of these religions and since people do not belong to more than one religion, we can project that all people and all souls go to Hell. With birth and death rates as they are, we can expect the number of souls in Hell to increase exponentially.

Now, we look at the rate of change of the volume in Hell because Boyle's Law states that in order for temperature and the pressure in Hell to stay the same, the volume of Hell has to expand as souls are added.

This gives two possibilities:

1. If Hell is expanding at a slower rate than the rate at which souls enter Hell, then the temperature and pressure in Hell will increase until all Hell breaks loose.

2. Of course, if Hell is expanding at a rate faster than the increase of souls in Hell, then the temperature and pressure will drop until Hell freezes over. So which is it? If we accept the postulate given to me by Ms Tracey Nicholson during my first year at uni – 'That it will be a cold night in Hell before I sleep with you' and take into account the fact that I still have not succeeded in that area, then (2) cannot be true, and so Hell is exothermic.'

This student got the only A.

〰〰〰〰

Never try to date a psychic; she'll leave before you meet.

Useful Work Phrases

Thank you. We're all refreshed and challenged by your unique point of view.

The fact that no one understands you doesn't mean you're an artist.

I don't know what your problem is, but I'll bet it's hard to pronounce.

Any connection between your reality and mine is purely coincidental.

I have plenty of talent and vision. I just don't care.

I like you. You remind me of when I was young and stupid.

I'm not being rude. You're just insignificant.

I'm already visualising the duct tape over your mouth.

I will always cherish the initial misconceptions I had about you.

It's a thankless job, but I've got a lot of karma to burn off.

Yes, I am an agent of Satan, but my duties are largely ceremonial.

No, my powers can only be used for good.

How about never? Is never good for you?

I'm really easy to get along with once you people learn to worship me.

You sound reasonable...Time to up my medication.

I'll try being nicer if you'll try being smarter.

I'm out of my mind, but feel free to leave me a message...

I don't work here. I'm a consultant.

Who me? I just wander from room to room.

My toys! My toys! I can't do this job without my toys!

It might look like I'm doing nothing, but at the cellular level I'm really quite busy.

At least I have a positive attitude about my destructive habits.

You are validating my inherent mistrust of strangers.

I see you've set aside this special time to humiliate yourself in public.

Someday, we'll look back on this, laugh nervously and change the subject.

〰〰〰〰

There are 24 hours in a day and 24 beers in a case...
coincidence?

10 Simple Rules for Dating My Daughter

Some thoughtful information for those who ARE daughters, WERE daughters, HAVE daughters, INTEND TO HAVE daughters, or INTEND TO DATE a daughter.

Rule One

If you pull into my driveway and honk, you'd better be delivering a package, because you're sure not picking anything up.

Rule Two

You do not touch my daughter in front of me. You may glance at her, so long as you do not peer at anything below her neck. If you cannot keep your eyes or hands off of my daughter's body, I will remove them.

Rule Three

I am aware that it is considered fashionable for boys of your age to wear their trousers so loosely that they appear to be falling off their hips. Please don't take this as an insult, but you and all of your friends are complete idiots. Still, I want to be fair and open minded about this issue, so I propose his compromise: You may come to the door with your underwear showing and your pants 10 sizes too big, and I will not object. However, in order to ensure that your clothes do not, in fact, come off during the course of your date with my daughter, I will take my electric nail gun and fasten your trousers securely in place to your waist.

Rule Four

I'm sure you've been told that in today's world, sex without utilising a 'barrier method' of some kind can kill you. Let me elaborate: when it comes to sex, I am the barrier, and I will kill you.

Rule Five

In order for us to get to know each other, you may think we should talk about sports, politics, and other issues of the day. Please do not do this. The only information I require from you is an indication of when you expect to have my daughter safely back at my house, and the only word I need from you on this subject is 'early'.

Rule Six

I have no doubt you are a popular fellow, with many opportunities to date other girls. This is fine with me as long as it is okay with my daughter. Otherwise, once you have gone out with my little girl, you will continue to date no one but her until she is finished with you. If you make her cry, I will make you cry.

Rule Seven

As you stand in my front hallway, waiting for my daughter to appear, and more than an hour goes by, do not sigh and fidget. If you want to be on time for the movie, you should not be dating. My daughter is putting on her makeup, a process that can take longer than painting the Sydney Harbour Bridge. Instead of just standing there, why don't you do something useful, like changing the oil in my car?

Rule Eight

The following places are not appropriate for a date with my daughter:

Places where there are beds, couches, or anything softer than a wooden stool.

Places where there are no parents, policemen or nuns within eyesight.

Places where there is darkness.

Places where there is dancing, holding hands, or happiness.

Places where the ambient temperature is warm enough to induce my daughter to wear shorts, tank tops, midriff T-shirts, or anything other than overalls, a jumper, and an arctic-grade jacket zipped up to her throat.

Football games are okay. Old folks homes are better.

Any movies with even the slightest of slight references to love, romance or sex must be avoided.

Movies which feature chainsaws are okay.

Rule Nine

Do not lie to me. I may appear to be a pot-bellied, balding, middle-aged, dim-witted has-been. But on issues relating to my daughter, I am the all-knowing, merciless God of your universe. If I ask you where you are going and with whom, you have one chance to tell me the truth, the whole truth and nothing but the truth. I have a shotgun, a shovel, and five acres behind the house. Do not trifle with me.

Rule Ten

Be afraid. Be very afraid. It takes very little for me to mistake the sound of your car in the driveway for a chopper coming in over a rice paddy outside of Hanoi. When my Agent Orange psychosis starts acting up, the voices in my head frequently tell me to clean the guns as I wait for you to bring my daughter home. As soon as you pull into the driveway you should exit your car with both hands in plain sight. Speak the perimeter password, announce in a clear voice that you have brought my daughter home safely and early, then return to your car – there is no need for you to come inside. The camouflaged face at the window is mine.

Canonical List of Oxymorons

Anarchy rules!

Thank God I'm an atheist

This page intentionally left blank

Act naturally

Airline food

Computer security

Constant change

Construction worker

Convenience store

Definite maybe

Diet ice-cream

Exact estimate

Fast food

Found missing

Fresh frozen

Good grief

Graduate student

Great Britain

Half dead

Happily married

Huge market niche

Journalistic integrity

Living dead

Married life

Mature student

Microsoft Works

Personal computer

Plastic glasses
Pretty ugly
Private email
Public school education
Quick fix
Rap music
Religious science
Resident alien
Safe sex
Same difference
Second best
Sensitive male
Silent scream
Smart bomb
Tax return
True story
Uncontested divorce

Coping With Stress

Jam miniature marshmallows up your nose and sneeze them out. See how many you can do at once.

Use your MasterCard to pay your Visa and vice-versa.

Pop some popcorn without putting the lid on.

When someone says 'Have a nice day', tell them you have other plans.
Make a list of things to do that you've already done.

Dance naked in front of your pets.

Put all your toddler's best clothes on backwards and send him off to pre-school as if nothing is out of the ordinary.

Fill out your tax forms using roman numerals.

Tape pictures of your boss on watermelons and launch them from high places.

Leaf through a *National Geographic* and draw underwear on the natives.

Tattoo 'out to lunch' on your forehead.

Go shopping. Buy everything. Sweat in it. Return it the next day.

Buy a subscription of *Sleezoid Weekly* and send it to your boss's wife.

Pay your electric bill in five-cent pieces.

Drive to work in reverse.

Tell your boss to 'blow it out of your mule' and let them figure it out.

Polish your car with ear wax.

Read the dictionary upside down and look for secret messages.

Start a nasty rumour and see if you recognise it when it comes back to you.

Braid the hairs in each nostril.

Write a short story using alphabet soup.

Stare at people through the tines of a fork and pretend they're in jail.

Make up a language and ask people for directions.

A Few Good Books

The Lion Attacked, Claude Yarmoff

How to Write Big Books, Warren Peace

The Art of Archery, Beau N. Arrow

Songs for Children, Barbara Blacksheep

Irish Heart Surgery, Angie O'Plasty

Split Personalities, Jacqueline Hyde

Under the Bleachers, Seymour Butts

Desert Crossing, I. Rhoda Camel

School Truancy, Marcus Absent

I Was a Cloakroom Attendant, Mahatma Coate

I Lost My Balance, Eileen Dover and Phil Down

Mystery in the Barnyard, Hu Flung Dung

Positive Reinforcement, Wade Ago

Shhh! Danielle Soloud

The Philippine Post Office, Imelda Letter

Things to Do at a Party, Bob Frapples

Stop Arguing, Xavier Breath

Come on In! Doris Open

The German Bank Robbery, Hans Zupp

I Hate the Sun, Gladys Knight

Prison Security, Barb Dweyer

Irish First Aid, R.U. O'Kaye

My Career as a Clown, Abe Ozo

The World's Deadliest Joke, Theophilus Punoval

Here's Pus in Your Eye, Lance Boyle

My Life on Skid Row, Titus A. Drum

I Didn't Do It! Ivan Alibi

Why I Eat at McDonalds, Tommy Ayk

I Hit the Wall, Isadore There

The Bruce Lee Story, Marsha Larts

Take This Job and Shove It, Ike Witt

Rapunzel Rapunzel, Harris Long

Split Personalities, Jacqueline Hyde

How I Won the Marathon, Randy Hoelway

Songs from 'South Pacific', Sam and Janet Evening

Things You Don't Want to Hear During Surgery

Better save that. We'll need it for the autopsy. Someone call the cleaner – we're going to need a mop.

Wait a minute, if this is his spleen, then what's that?

Hand me that... uh... that uh... thingie.

Oops! Hey, has anyone ever survived 500 ml of this stuff before?

Rats, there go the lights again...

Ya know, there's big money in kidneys. Heck, the guy's got two of 'em.

Everybody stand back! I lost my contact lens!

Could you stop that thing from beating? It's throwing my concentration off!

What's this doing here?

That's cool! Now can you make his leg twitch?

I wish I hadn't forgotten my glasses.

Well, folks, this will be an experiment for all of us.

Sterile, schmerile. The floor's clean, right?

Anyone see where I left that scalpel?

OK, now take a picture from this angle. This is truly a freak of nature.

Nurse, did this patient sign the organ donation card?

Don't worry. I think it is sharp enough.

She's gonna blow! Everyone take cover!

Rats! Page 47 of the manual is missing!

FIRE! FIRE! Everyone get out!

5 Questions Most Feared by Men

1. What are you thinking about?
2. Do you love me?
3. Do I look fat?
4. Do you think she is prettier than me?
5. What would you do if I died?

Tech Support

Dear Tech Support,
Last year I upgraded from Girlfriend 7.0 to Wife 1.0 and noticed that the new program began unexpected child processing that took up a lot of new space and valuable resources. No mention of this phenomenon was included in the product brochure.

In addition, Wife 1.0 installs itself into all other programs and launches during system initialisation, where it monitors all other system activity. Applications such as Poker Night 10.3, Drunken Boys Night

2.5 and Saturday Football 5.0 no longer run, crashing the system whenever selected.

I cannot seem to keep Wife 1.0 in the background while attempting to run some of my other favourite applications. I am thinking about going back to Girlfriend 7.0, but the uninstall does not work on this program.

> Can you please help me !!!???
> Thanks,
> A Troubled User

Excuses for Missing Work

If it is all the same to you I won't be coming in to work. The voices told me to clean all the guns today.

I set half the clocks in my house ahead an hour and the other half back an hour Saturday and spent 18 hours in some freaky kind of space-time continuum loop, reliving Sunday (right up until the explosion). I was able to exit the loop only by reversing the polarity of the power source in the house, while simultaneously rapping my dog on the snout with a rolled up newspaper. Accordingly, I will be in late, or early.

I can't come in to work today because I'll be stalking my previous boss, who fired me for not showing up for work.

Yes, I seem to have contracted some attention-deficit disorder and, hey, how about that game Saturday night, huh? So, I won't be able to, yes, could I help you? No, no, I'll be sticking with my existing telecommunications carrier, but thank you for calling.

Constipation has made me a walking time bomb. I just found out that I was switched at birth. Legally, I shouldn't come to work knowing my employee records may now contain false information.

The psychiatrist said it was an excellent session. He even gave me this jaw restraint so I won't bite things when I am startled.

The dog ate my car keys. We're going to hitchhike to the vet.

I prefer to remain an enigma.

My stepmother has come back as one of the undead and we must track her to her coffin to drive a stake through her heart and give her eternal peace. One day should do it.

I am converting my calendar from Julian to Gregorian.

I am extremely sensitive to a rise in the interest rates.

I've used up all my sick days... so I'm calling in dead!

Ways to be Offensive at a Funeral

Tell the widow that the deceased's last wish was that she have sex with you.

Tell the undertaker that he can't close the coffin until you find your contact lens.

Punch the body and tell people he hit you first.

Tell the widow that you're the deceased's gay lover.

Ask someone to take a snapshot of you shaking hands with the deceased.

At the cemetary, play taps on a kazoo.

Walk around telling people that you've seen the will and they're not in it.

Drive behind the widow's limousine and keep honking your horn.

Tell the undertaker that your dog just died and ask him if he can sneak him into the coffin.

Place a hard-boiled egg into the mouth of the deceased.

Walk around telling people that the deceased didn't like them.

Use the deceased's tongue to lick a stamp.

Ask the widow for money which the deceased owes you.

The Biggest Lies

The cheque is in the mail.

I'll respect you in the morning.

I'm from your government, and I am here to help you.

It's only a cold sore.

You get this one, I'll pay next time.

My wife doesn't understand me.

Trust me, I'll take care of everything.

Of course I love you.

I am getting a divorce.

Drinking? Why, no, Officer.

It's not the money, it's the principle of the thing.
...but we can still be good friends.

She means nothing to me.

Don't worry, he's never bitten anyone.

I'll call you later.

I've never done anything like this before.

Now, I'm going to tell you the truth.

It's supposed to make that noise.

...then take a left. You can't miss it.

Yes, I did.

Thoughts to Get You Through Almost Any Crisis

Insanity is hereditary – you get it from your kids.

There is absolutely no substitute for a genuine lack of preparation.

Happiness is merely the remission of pain and absence of worry.

Nostalgia isn't what it used to be.

The facts, although interesting, are irrelevant.

The careful application of terror is also a form of communication.

Someone who thinks logically provides a nice contrast to the real world.

Things are more like they are today then they have ever been before.

Anything worth fighting for is worth fighting dirty for.

Everything should be made as simple as possible but no simpler.

Friends may come and go, and indeed they do, but enemies accumulate.

I have seen the truth and it makes no sense.

Suicide is the most sincere form of self-criticism.

If you think that there is good in everybody, you haven't met everybody.

All things being equal, fat people use more soap.

If you can smile when things go wrong, you have someone in mind to blame.

One-seventh of your life is spent on Monday.

By the time you can make ends meet, they move the ends.

Not one shred of evidence supports the notion that life is serious.

There is always one more imbecile than you counted on.

Never wrestle with a pig. You both get dirty and the pig likes it.

∿∿∿∿∿

I am not a perfectionist. But I'm happy to say my parents were.

∿∿∿∿∿

Many people stop looking for work when they find a job.

∿∿∿∿∿

Talk is cheap because supply exceeds demand.

Ways to be Annoying

Practise the art of limp handshakes.

Tell the ending of movies.

Blow out other people's birthday candles.

When giving directions, leave out a turn or two.

Before exiting the elevator, push all the buttons, including the buttons on the emergency phone.

Draw moustaches on posters.

Bite your dentist's finger.

Dance fast to slow music and vice-versa.

Tell people they have bad breath.

Smell smoke often and announce it.

Eat out at an expensive restaurant with friends and 'forget' your wallet.

Put everyone on speakerphone.

Step on the back of the shoe of the person in front of you.

Make scary faces at babies.

Flirt with a friend's spouse.

Pretend you're listening.

Shake with your left hand.

Love and Sex

The more beautiful the woman is who loves you, the easier it is to leave her with no hard feelings.

Nothing improves with age.

No matter how many times you've had it, if it's offered take it, because it'll never be quite the same again.

Sex has no calories.

Sex takes up the least amount of time and causes the most amount of trouble.

There is no remedy for sex but more sex.

Sex appeal is 50% what you've got and 50% what people think you've got.

Sex is like snow: you never know how many inches you are going to get or how long it is going to last.

A man in the house is worth two in the street.

If you get them by the balls, their hearts and minds will follow.

Virginity can be cured.

When a man's wife learns to understand him, she usually stops listening to him.

Never sleep with anyone crazier than yourself.

The qualities that most attract a woman to a man

are the same ones she can't stand years later.

It is always the wrong time of month.

When the lights are out, all women are beautiful.

Sex is hereditary. If your parents never had it, chances are you won't either.

Sow your wild oats on Saturday night – then on Sunday pray for crop failure.

The younger the better.

The game of love is never called off on account of darkness.

It was not the apple on the tree but the pair on the ground that caused the trouble in the garden.

Sex discriminates against the shy and the ugly.

Before you find your handsome prince, you've got to kiss a lot of frogs.

There may be some things better than sex, and some things worse than sex. But there is nothing exactly like it.

Love your neighbor, but don't get caught.

Love is a hole in the heart.

Love is a matter of chemistry, sex is a matter of physics.

Do it only with the best.

Sex is a three-letter word which needs some old-fashioned four-letter words to convey its full meaning.

One good turn gets most of the blankets.

You cannot produce a baby in one month by impregnating nine women.

Love is the triumph of imagination over intelligence.

It is better to have loved and lost than never to have loved at all.

Thou shalt not commit adultery... unless in the mood.

Never lie down with a woman who's got more troubles than you.

Abstain from wine, women, and song; mostly song.

Never argue with a women when she's tired – or rested.

A woman never forgets the men she could have had; a man, the women he couldn't.

What matters is not the length of the wand, but the magic in the stick.

It is better to be looked over than overlooked.

Never say no.

A man can be happy with any woman as long as he doesn't love her.

Folks playing leapfrog must complete all jumps.

Beauty is skin deep; ugly goes right to the bone.

A man is only a man, but a good bicycle is a ride.

Love comes in spurts.

Sex is one of the nine reasons for reincarnation; the other eight are unimportant.

Smile, it makes people wonder what you are thinking.

Don't do it if you can't keep it up.

There is no difference between a wise man and a fool when they fall in love.

Never go to bed mad. Stay up and fight.

Love is the delusion that one woman differs from another.

~~~~~~~

Love defenceless animals, especially in a good gravy.

~~~~~~~

Beauty is in the eye of the beer holder.

Memo to All Employees

New Company Policies: Sickness and Related Leave

We will no longer accept a doctor's statement as proof of sickness. If you are able to go to the doctor, you are able to come to work.

Surgery: Operations are now banned. As long as you are an employee here, you need all your organs. You should not consider removing anything. We hired you intact. To have something removed constitutes a breach of employment.

Your Own Death: This will be accepted as an excuse. However, we require at least two weeks notice as it is your duty to train your replacement.

Bathroom Use: Entirely too much time is being spent in the rest room. In the future, we will follow the practice of going in alphabetical order. For instance, those whose names begin with 'A' will go from 8:00 to 8:10, employees whose names begin with 'B' will go from 8:10 to 8:20 and so on. If you're unable to go at your time, it will be necessary to wait until the next day when your time comes again. In extreme emergencies employees may swap their time with a co-worker. Both employees' supervisors must approve this exchange in writing. In addition, there is now a strict three-minute time limit in the cubicle. At the end of three minutes, an alarm bell will sound, the toilet paper roll will retract, and the cubicle door will open.

Romance Points System

In the world of romance, one single rule applies: make the woman happy. Do something she likes, and you get points. Do something she dislikes and points are subtracted. You don't get any points for doing something she expects. Sorry, that's the way the game is played. Here is a guide to the points system:

Simple Duties

You leave the toilet seat up   -5

You replace the toilet paper roll when it is empty 0

When the toilet paper roll is barren, you resort to Kleenex   -1

When the Kleenex runs out you use the next bathroom   -2

You go out to buy her extra-light panty liners with wings   +5

In the snow   +8

...but return with beer   -5

...and no panty liners   -25

You check out a suspicious noise at night 0

You check out a suspicious noise and it is nothing 0

You check out a suspicious noise and it is
something +5

You pummel it with a six iron +10

It's her cat -40

Social Engagements
You stay by her side the entire party 0

You stay by her side for a while, then leave to
chat with a college drinking buddy -2
...named Tiffany -4

Tiffany is a dancer -6
...with breast implants -18

Her Birthday
You take her out to dinner 0

You take her out to dinner and it's not a sports
bar +1

Okay, it is a sports bar -2

And it's all-you-can-eat night -3

It's a sports bar, it's all-you-can-eat night, and
your face is painted the colours of your
favourite team -10

A Night Out with the Boys

Go with a pal	-5
The pal is happily married	-4
Or frighteningly single	-7
And he drives a Mustang	-10
And his name is Kingo	-45

A Night Out

You take her to a movie	+2
You take her to a movie she likes	+4
You take her to a movie you hate	+6
You take her to a movie you like	-2
It's called Death Cop 3	-3
...which features Cyborgs that eat humans	-9
You lied and said it was a foreign film about orphans	-15

Your Physique

You develop a noticeable pot belly	-15
You develop a noticeable pot belly and exercise to get rid of it	+10
You develop a noticeable pot belly and resort to loose jeans and baggy Hawaiian shirts	-30
You say, 'It doesn't matter, you have one too.'	-800

The Big Question
She asks, 'Do I look fat?'

You hesitate in responding	-10
You reply, 'Where?'	-35
Any other response	-20

Communication
When she wants to talk about a problem:

You listen, displaying a concerned expression	0
You listen, for over 30 minutes	+5
You listen for more than 30 minutes without looking at the TV	+100
She realises this is because you have fallen asleep	-200

~~~~~~~~~

If you choke a smurf, what colour does it turn?

~~~~~~~~~

*What happens if you get scared half to death...
twice?*

~~~~~~~~~

My inferiority complex is not as good as yours.

Why Bicycles Are Better Than Women

Bicycles don't get pregnant.

You can ride your bicycle any time of the month.

Bicycles don't have parents.

Bicycles don't whine unless something is really wrong.

You can share your bicycle with your friends.

Bicycles don't care how many other bicycles you've ridden.

When riding, you and your bicycle can arrive at the same time.

Bicycles don't care how many other bicycles you have.

Bicycles don't care if you look at other bicycles.

Bicycles don't care if you buy bicycle magazines.

If your bicycle goes flat you can fix it.

If your bicycle is too loose you can tighten it.

You don't have to be jealous of the guy who works on your bicycle.

If you say bad things to your bicycle, you don't have to apologise before you ride it again.

Why Bicycles Are Better Than Men

Bicycles don't work late.

Your bicycle stays as clean as you want it to.

Bicycles don't have parents.

Bicycles don't get sick.

Bicycles don't get overweight, except as per your convenience.

You can check out the guy who works on your bicycle.

Your bicycle always has time for you.

Bicycles don't complain and don't ride away from you when the road gets rough.

Bicycles don't watch TV.

Bicycles don't shave.

Bicycles don't snore.

Bicycles don't leave a mess in the kitchen or bathroom.

Bicycles are better protection in a bad neighbourhood.

If you don't like the size of your bicycle you can get a new one.

You can ride your bicycle as long as you want and it won't get sore.

You can stop riding your bicycle as soon as you want and it won't get frustrated.

Your parents won't remain in touch with your old bicycle after you dump it.

Bicycles don't get headaches.

Bicycles don't insult you if you're a bad rider.

Your bicycle never wants a night out with the other bicycles.

Bicycles don't care if you're late.

You don't have to take a shower before you ride your bicycle.

If your bicycle doesn't look good you can paint it or get better parts.

You can ride your bicycle the first time you meet it, without having to take it to dinner, see a movie, or meet its mother.

The only protection you have to wear when riding your bicycle is a decent helmet.

When in mixed company, you can talk about what a great ride you had the last time you were on your bicycle.

You can try out as many bikes as you like before you get your own.

You don't have to feed your bicycle.

Bicycles never argue, you are always right.

Bicycles never wake you up in the middle of the night, for any reason.

Bicycles never try to show you off to their friends.

Bicycles don't sneak around with other bicycles.

Bicycles don't care what you look like or what your age is.

Bicycles don't care and don't comment about what you spend your money on.

When you go riding, your bicycle doesn't care if other bicycles are bigger or better.

Bicycles don't care about their performance.

Bicycles don't get you pregnant.

When you've finished a ride, you can get off.

You don't have to praise a bike after a ride.

Bicycles don't sulk.

Bicycles don't bore you.

Bicycles don't abandon you at gatherings for more interesting riders.

Bicycles don't have to prove anything.

Bicycles don't try to change you once you've bought them.

Bicycles never interrogate you.

Bicycles don't fart in bed.

Bicycles don't leave smelly inner tubes lying around on the floor.

Second-hand bikes don't brag about previous owners.

Second-hand bikes don't go to see previous owners for a ride when you're out of town.

You don't have to explain to a bike if you don't feel like a ride.

Guide to Safe Fax

Q. Do I have to be married to have safe fax?
A. Although married people fax quite often, there are many single people who fax complete and utter strangers every day.

Q. My parents say they never had fax when they were young and were only allowed to write memos to each other until they turned 21. How old do you think someone should be before they can fax?

A. Faxing can be performed at any age, once you learn the correct procedure.

Q. If I fax by myself will I go blind?
A. Certainly not, as far as we can see.

Q. There is a place on our street where you can go and pay for fax. Is this legal?
A. Yes, many people have no outlet for their fax needs and must pay a 'professional'.

Q. Should a cover always be used for faxing?
A. Unless you are really sure of the one you are faxing, a cover sheet should always be used to ensure safe fax.

Q. What happens when I incorrectly perform the procedure, and I fax prematurely?
A. Don't panic. Many people prematurely fax when they haven't faxed in a long time. Just start all over. Most people won't mind if you try again.

Q. I have a personal and a business fax. Can the transmission become mixed up?
A. Being bi-faxual can be confusing, but as long as you use a cover with each one, you shouldn't transmit anything you're not supposed to.

10 Ways to Terrorise a Telemarketer

When they ask 'How are you today?', tell them! 'I'm so glad you asked because no one these days seems to care, and I have all these problems; my arthritis is acting up, my eyelashes are sore, my dog just died...'

If they say they're John Doe from XYZ Company, ask them to spell their name. Then ask them to spell the company name. Then ask them where it is located. Continue asking them personal questions or questions about their company for as long as necessary.

Cry out in surprise, 'Judy! Is that you? Oh my God! Judy, how have you been?' Hopefully, this will give Judy a few brief moments of pause as she tries to figure out where she could know you from.

Tell the telemarketer you are on 'home incarceration' and ask if they could bring you a slab of beer and some chips.

After the telemarketer gives their spiel, ask him or her to marry you. When they get all flustered, tell them that you could not just give your credit card number to a complete stranger.

Tell the telemarketer you are busy at the moment and ask them if they will give you their *home* phone number so you can call them back. When the telemarketer explains that they cannot give out their home number, you say, 'I guess you don't want anyone bothering you at home, right?' The telemarketer will agree and you say, 'Now you know how I feel!' Say goodbye – and hang up.

Insist that the caller is really your buddy Leon, playing a joke. 'Come on Leon, cut it out! Seriously, Leon, how's your mum?'

Tell them to talk v-e-r-y s-l-o-w-l-y, because you want to write every word down.

For Those Who Take Life Too Seriously

On the other hand, you have different fingers.

I just got lost in thought. It was unfamiliar territory.

42.7 percent of all statistics are made up on the spot.

99 percent of lawyers give the rest a bad name.

I feel like I'm diagonally parked in a parallel universe.

You have the right to remain silent. Anything you say will be misquoted, then used against you.

I wonder how much deeper the ocean would be without sponges.

Remember, half the people you know are below average.

Despite the cost of living, have you noticed how popular it remains?

Nothing is foolproof to a talented fool.

Eagles may soar, but weasels don't get sucked into jet engines.

The early bird may get the worm, but the second mouse gets the cheese.

I drive way too fast to worry about cholesterol.

If Barbie is so popular, why do you have to buy her friends?

The only substitute for good manners is fast reflexes.

Support bacteria – they're the only culture some people have.

When everything's coming your way, you're in the wrong lane and going the wrong way.

A conclusion is the place where you got tired of thinking.

Experience is something you don't get until just after you need it.

For every action there is an equal and opposite criticism.

Bills travel through the mail at twice the speed of cheques.

No one is listening until you make a mistake.

Success always occurs in private and failure in full view.

The colder the x-ray table the more of your body is required on it.

The hardness of butter is directly proportional to the softness of the bread.

The severity of the itch is inversely proportional to the ability to reach it.

To steal ideas from one person is plagiarism; to steal from many is research.

Two wrongs are only the beginning.

The sooner you fall behind the more time you'll have to catch up.

A clear conscience is usually the sign of a bad memory.

Change is inevitable except from vending machines.

Plan to be spontaneous – tomorrow.

If you think nobody cares, try missing a couple of payments.

Honk if you love peace and quiet.

Beer Troubleshooting

SYMPTOM: Beer unusually pale and tasteless.
FAULT: Glass empty.
ACTION: Get someone to buy you another beer.

SYMPTOM: Opposite wall covered with fluorescent lights.
FAULT: You have fallen over backwards.
ACTION: Have yourself leashed to bar.

SYMPTOM: Mouth contains cigarette butts.
FAULT: You have fallen forward.
ACTION: See above.

SYMPTOM: Can't taste beer, front of your shirt is wet.
FAULT: Mouth not open, or glass applied to wrong part of face.
ACTION: Retire to restroom, practise in mirror.

SYMPTOM: Floor blurred.
FAULT: You are looking through bottom of empty glass.
ACTION: Get someone to buy you another beer.

SYMPTOM: Floor moving.
FAULT: You are being carried out.
ACTION: Find out if you are being taken to another bar.

SYMPTOM: Room seems unusually dark.
FAULT: Bar has closed.
ACTION: Confirm home address with bartender.

SYMPTOM: Taxi suddenly takes on colourful textures and aspect.
FAULT: Beer consumption has exceeded personal limitations.
ACTION: Cover mouth.

SYMPTOM: Everyone looks up to you and smiles.
FAULT: You are dancing on the table.
ACTION: Fall on somebody cushy-looking.

SYMPTOM: Beer is crystal-clear.
FAULT: It's water. Someone is trying to sober you up.
ACTION: Punch him.

SYMPTOM: Hands hurt, nose hurts, mind unusually clear.
FAULT: You have been in a fight.
ACTION: Apologise to everyone you see, just in case it was them.

SYMPTOM: Don't recognise anyone, don't recognise the room you're in.
FAULT: You've wandered into the wrong party.
ACTION: See if they have free beer.

SYMPTOM: Your singing sounds distorted.

FAULT: The beer is too weak.

ACTION: Have more beer until your voice improves.

SYMPTOM: Don't remember the words to the song.

FAULT: Beer is just right.

ACTION: Play air guitar.

Words of Wisdom

A man will pay $2.00 for a $1.00 item he needs.

A woman will pay $1.00 for a $2.00 item that she does not need.

A woman worries about the future until she gets a husband.

A man never worries about the future until he gets a wife.

A successful man is one who makes more money than his wife can spend.

A successful woman is one who can find such a man.

To be happy with a man, you must love him a little and understand him a lot.

To be happy with a woman you must love her a lot and not try to understand her at all.

Men wake up as good-looking as they went to bed. Women somehow deteriorate overnight.

A woman marries a man expecting he will change, but he doesn't.

A man marries a woman expecting she won't change, but she does.

Married men live longer than single men, but married men are more willing to die.

A woman has the last word in any argument.

Anything a man says after that is the beginning of a new argument.

Gender Dictionary

Butt
female: The body part that every item of clothing manufactured makes 'look bigger'.

male: The organ used for mooning (and farting).

Commitment
female: A desire to get married and raise a family.

male: Not trying to pick up other women while out with one's girlfriend.

Communication

female: The open sharing of thoughts and feelings with one's partner.

male: Scratching out a note before suddenly taking off for a weekend with the guys.

Flatulence

female: An embarrassing by-product of digestion.

male: An endless source of entertainment, self-expression and male bonding.

Lesbian

female: A woman who makes love to other women.

male: A woman who has sex with other women so men can watch and get really turned on.

Making love

female: The greatest expression of intimacy a couple can achieve.

male: What men have to call boinking to get women to boink.

Remote control

female: A device for changing from one TV channel to another.

male: A device for scanning through all channels every three minutes.

Taste

female: Something you do frequently to whatever you're cooking, to make sure it's good.

male: Something you must do to anything you think has gone bad, prior to tossing it out.

Thingy

female: Any part under a car's hood.

male: The strap fastener on a woman's bra.

Vulnerable

female: Fully opening up one's self emotionally to another.

male: Playing cricket without a box.

Wants & needs

female: The delicate balance of emotional, physical and psychological longing one seeks to have fulfilled in a relationship.

male: Food, sex and beer.

~~~~~~~~

I plan on living forever. So far, so good.

~~~~~~~~

If you can't repair your brakes, make your horn louder.

Questions Not to Ask in a Job Interview

What's your company's policy on severance pay?

How long does it take your company's bureaucracy to get around to firing somebody for poor performance?

Does your company's life insurance cover suicide?

Who's the ugly bitch in that picture on your desk?

Does your company's insurance consider genital herpes a pre-existing condition?

How many sick days do you allow each employee before you stop paying them for not being here?

Does your insurance cover sex-change operations?

Does your LAN have a firewall that blocks triple-X websites?

How frequently do your accountants audit petty cash?

~~~~~~~~

Shin: a device for finding furniture in the dark.

~~~~~~~~

Why do psychics have to ask you for your name?

Things Men Know

Men know that Mother Nature's best aphrodisiac is still a naked woman.

Men know that PMS is Mother Nature's way of telling you to get out of the house.

Men know that cats are evil and cannot be trusted.

Men know how to change the toilet paper, but to do so would ruin the game.

Men know that from time to time, it is absolutely necessary to adjust oneself.

Men know that a woman will wear a low-cut dress and expect the man to stare at her cleavage. Men also know that the woman will get pissed off when they do, for reasons not totally clear to them.

Men know that it's never a good idea to tell your father-in-law how good his daughter is in bed.

Men know that men are from here, and women are from way the hell over there.

~~~~~~~~

A day without sunshine is like night.

~~~~~~~~

Conscience is what hurts when everything else feels so good.

Things Only Women Understand

Cats' facial expressions.

The need for the same style of shoes in different colours.

Fat clothes.

Fat mirrors.

Taking a car trip without trying to beat your best time.

The difference between beige, off-white, and eggshell.

Eyelash curlers.

The inaccuracy of every bathroom scale ever made.

Other women.

Ways to Stay Stressed

Never exercise. Exercise wastes a lot of time that could be spent worrying.

Eat anything you like. Hey, if cigarette smoke can't cleanse your system, a balanced diet isn't likely to.

Gain weight. Work hard at staying at least 10 kilos over your recommended weight.

Take plenty of stimulants. The old standards of caffeine, nicotine, sugar, and cola will continue to do the job just fine.

Avoid 'woo-hoo' practices. Ignore the evidence suggesting that meditation, yoga, deep breathing, and/or mental imaging help to reduce stress. The Protestant work ethic is good for everyone, Protestant or not.

Get rid of your social support system. Let the few friends who are willing to tolerate you know that you concern yourself with friendships only if you have time, and you never have time. If a few people persist in trying to be your friend, avoid them.

Personalise all criticism. Anyone who criticises any aspect of your work, family, dog, house, or car is mounting a personal attack. Don't take time to listen – be offended, and then return the attack!

Males and females alike – be macho. Never ask for help, and if you want it done right, do it yourself!

*Become a workaholic.*Put work before everything else, and be sure to take work home evenings and weekends. Keep reminding yourself that holidays are for sissies.

Discard good time management skills. Schedule in more activities every day than you can possibly get done and then worry about it all whenever you get a chance.

Procrastinate. Putting things off to the last second always produces a marvellous amount of stress.

Worry about things you can't control Worry about the stock market, earthquakes, the approaching Ice Age, you know, all the big issues.

Become not only a perfectionist but set impossibly high standards... and either beat yourself up, or feel guilty, depressed, discouraged, and/or inadequate when you don't meet them.

Throw out your sense of humour. Staying stressed is no laughing matter so don't treat it as one.

Signs You Have a Drinking Problem

You lose arguments with inanimate objects.

You have to hold onto the lawn to keep from falling off the earth.

Work starts interfering with your drinking.

Your doctor finds traces of blood in your alcohol system.

The back of your head keeps getting hit by the toilet seat.

You sincerely believe alcohol to be the elusive fifth food group.

That damned pink elephant followed you home again.

You believe 'Two hands and just one mouth... that's a drinking problem'.

You can focus better with one eye closed.

Every woman you see has an exact twin.

You fall off the floor or up the stairs.

You discover in the morning that your liquid cleaning supplies have mysteriously disappeared.

Five beers has just as many kilojoules as a burger, so you skip dinner.

Beer: it's not just for breakfast any more.

The glass keeps missing your mouth.

When you go to donate blood they ask what proof it is.

Mosquitoes and vampires get a buzz after biting you.

You believe your only drinking problem is not having a drink right now.

At AA meetings you begin: 'Hi, my name is... uh...'

Having a hard time staying on the footpath because you walk in the pattern of left, right, stumble, fall.

You tell people, 'I'm not under the affluence of incohol.'

You wake up with a traffic cone between your legs.

When you tell people, 'I'm not drunk... You're just sober.'

When the bar owner carves your name onto your own barstool.

Women's Guide to Driving Men Crazy

Do not say what you mean. Ever.

Be ambiguous. Always.

Cry. Cry often.

Bring things up that were said, done, or thought years, months, or decades ago... or with other boyfriends.

Make them apologise for everything.

Stash feminine products in their cars, backpacks and in their books as cute reminders that you were thinking of them.

Look them in the eye and start laughing.

Get mad at them for everything.

Discuss your period in front of them. Watch them squirm.

Demand to be called or emailed. Often. Whine when they don't comply.

When complimented, make sure to be paranoid.

Take nothing at face value.

Use daddy as a weapon. Tell them about his gun collection, his quick trigger finger, and his affection for his Little Princess.

Be late for everything. Yell if they're late.

Talk about your ex-boyfriend 24 hours a day, seven days a week. Compare and contrast.

Make them guess what you want and then get mad when they're wrong.

Plan little relationship anniversaries, eg the monthly anniversary of the time you saw each other in the library. Then get mad at them for forgetting. Then cry.

Gather many female friends and dance to 'I Will Survive' while they are present. Sing all the words. Sing to them. Sing loud.

Constantly claim you're fat. Ask them. Then cry, regardless of their answer.

Leave out the good parts in stories.

Make them wonder. Confusion is a good thing.

Criticise the way they dress.

Criticise the music they listen to.

When asked, 'What's wrong?' tell them that if they don't know, you're not going to tell them.

Try to change them.

Try to mould them.

Try to get them to dance.

When they screw up, never let them forget it.

Blame everything on PMS.

Whenever there is silence ask them, 'What are you thinking?'

Read into everything.

Over-analyse everything.

Things to Say When Caught Napping at Your Desk

'They said at the blood bank this might happen.'

'This is just a 15-minute power-nap like they raved about in the last time management course you sent me to.'

'Whew! Guess I left the top off the liquid paper.'

'I wasn't sleeping! I was meditating on the mission statement and envisioning a new paradigm!'

'This is one of the seven habits of highly effective people!'

'I was testing the keyboard for drool resistance.'

'I'm actually doing a Stress Level Elimination Exercise Plan (S.L.E.E.P.) I learned at the last mandatory seminar you made me attend.'

'I was doing a highly specific yoga exercise to relieve work-related stress. Are you discriminatory towards people who practise yoga?'

'Damn! Why did you interrupt me? I had almost figured out a solution to our biggest problem.'

'Boy, that cold medicine I took last night just won't wear off!'

'Ah, the unique and unpredictable circadian rhythms of the workaholic!'

'Wasn't sleeping. Was trying to pick up contact lens without hands.'

'Amen.'

~~~~~~~~

Black holes are where God divided by zero.

Things That Guys Wished Girls Knew

If you think you're fat, you probably are. Don't ask us.

Learn to work the toilet seat: if it's up, put it down.

Birthdays, Valentine's Day and anniversaries are not quests to see if we can find the perfect present, again!

If you ask a question you don't want an answer to, expect an answer you don't want to hear.

Sometimes, we're not thinking about you. Live with it.

Get rid of your cat. No, it's not different. It's just like every other cat.

Dogs are better than cats. Period.

Your brother is an idiot, your ex-boyfriend is an idiot, and your dad probably is too.

Ask for what you want. Subtle hints don't work.

Yes, pissing standing up is more difficult than peeing from point blank range. We're bound to miss sometimes.

Yes and no are perfectly acceptable answers.

A headache that lasts seven months is a problem. See a doctor.

173

Your mum doesn't have to be our best friend.

It is neither in your best interest nor ours to take 'the quiz' from *Cosmopolitan* together.

Anything we said six or eight months ago is inadmissible in an argument. All comments become null and void after 24 hours.

If something we say can be interpreted two ways, and one of the ways makes you sad or angry, we meant the other one.

Don't rub the lamp if you don't want the genie to come out.

You can either ask us to do something or tell us how you want it done. But asking us to do both is only going to cause trouble.

Women wearing Wonderbras and low-cut blouses lose their right to complain about having their boobs stared at.

Telling us that the models in the men's magazines are airbrushed makes you look jealous and petty and it's not going to deter us from reading the magazines.

The relationship is never going to be like it was the first two months we were going out.

Cat Wisdom

Cats do what they want, when they want.

They rarely listen to you.

They're totally unpredictable.

They whine when they are not happy.

When you want to play they want to be alone.

When you want to be alone, they want to play.

They expect you to cater to their every whim.

They're moody.

They leave hair everywhere.

They drive you nuts.

Conclusion: they're like little, tiny women in cheap fur coats.

The Little Things That Drive a Sane Person Mad

You have to try on a pair of sunglasses with that stupid little plastic thing in the middle of them.

The person behind you in the supermarket runs his trolley into the back of your ankle.

The elevator stops on every floor and nobody gets on.

There's always a car riding your tail when you're slowing down to find an address.

You open a can of soup and the lid falls in.

It's bad enough that you step in dog mess, but you don't realise it till you walk across your living room rug.

The tiny red string on the Band-Aid wrapper never works for you.

There's a dog in the neighbourhood that barks at everything.

You can never put anything back in a box the way it came.

You drink from a can into which someone has extinguished a cigarette.

You slice your tongue licking an envelope.

Your tyre gauge lets out half the air while you're trying to get a reading.

A station comes in brilliantly when you're standing near the radio but buzzes, drifts and spits every time you move away.

There are always one or two ice cubes that won't pop out of the tray.

You wash a garment with a tissue in the pocket and your entire laundry comes out covered with lint.

You set the alarm on your digital clock for 7 pm instead of 7 am.

The radio station doesn't tell you who sang that song.

You rub on hand cream and can't turn the bathroom doorknob to get out.

People behind you on a supermarket line dash ahead of you to a counter just opening up.

Your glasses slide off your ears when you perspire.

You can't look up the correct spelling of a word in the dictionary because you don't know how to spell it.

You have to inform five different sales people in the same store that you're just browsing.

You had that pen in your hand only a second ago and now you can't find it.

You reach under the table to pick something off the floor and smash your head on the way up.

~~~~~~~~

If you try to fail, and succeed, which have you done?

~~~~~~~~

Technology is simply a means of manipulating the world so you don't have to experience it.

'Why Aren't You Married?' Snappy Comebacks

You haven't asked yet.

I was hoping to do something meaningful with my life.

What? And spoil my great sex life?

Nobody would believe me in white.

Just lucky, I guess.

It gives my mother something to live for.

My fiance is awaiting parole.

I'm waiting until I get to be your age.

It didn't seem worth a blood test.

I already have enough laundry to do, thank you.

Because I think it would take all the spontaneity out of dating.

I'd have to forfeit my billion-dollar trust fund.

They just opened a great singles bar down the street.

I wouldn't want my parents to drop dead from sheer happiness.

We really want to, but my lover's husband just won't go for it.

Why aren't you thin?

Reasons to Study Martial Arts

Broken masonry makes great drainage for potted plants.

You get beaten up by people half your size and twice your age.

You'll never run out of kindling wood again.

There is no need to wonder what belt to wear.

You get to be on first name basis with the emergency room staff.

The uniforms make nice pyjamas.

You get to appreciate the finer points of Chuck Norris's acting.

You learn to count to 10 in three different Asian languages.

~~~~~~~~

If at first you do succeed,
try not to look too astonished.

~~~~~~~~

A meeting is an event at which the minutes are kept
and the hours are lost.

Baby Boomers – Now and Then

Then: Killer Weed.
Now: Weed Killer.

Then: Being caught with Hustler magazine.
Now: Being caught by Hustler magazine.

Then: Getting out to a new, hip joint.
Now: Getting a new hip joint.

Then: Being called into the principal's office.
Now: Storming into the principal's office.

Then: Peace Sign.
Now: Mercedes Logo.

Then: 'Going blind.'
Now: Really going blind.

Then: Long hair.
Now: Longing for hair.

Then: Worrying about no one coming to your party.

Now: Worrying about no one coming to your funeral.

Then: The perfect high.
Now: The perfect high-yield mutual fund.

Then: Swallowing acid.
Now: Swallowing antacid.

Then: You're growing pot.
Now: Your growing pot.

Then: Passing the driving test.
Now: Passing the vision test.

Then: Seeds and stems.
Now: Roughage.

Then: Popping pills, smoking joints.
Now: Popping joints.

Then: Ommmmmm.
Now: Ummmmm.

Secrets of Personal Growth

As I let go of my feelings of guilt, I am in touch with my inner sociopath.

I have the power to channel my imagination into ever-soaring levels of suspicion and paranoia.

I assume full responsibility for my actions, except the ones that are someone else's fault.

I no longer need to punish, deceive, or compromise myself, unless I want to stay employed.

In some cultures what I do would be considered normal.

Having control over myself is almost as good as having control over others.

My intuition nearly makes up for my lack of self-judgement.

I honour my personality flaws for without them I would have no personality at all.

Joan of Arc heard voices too.

I am grateful that I am not as judgemental as all those censorious, self-righteous people around me.

I need not suffer in silence while I can still moan, whimper, and complain.

As I learn the innermost secrets of people around me, they reward me in many ways to keep me quiet.

When someone hurts me, I know that forgiveness is cheaper than a lawsuit, but not nearly as gratifying.

The first step is to say nice things about myself. The second, to do nice things for myself. The third, to find someone to buy me nice things.

As I learn to trust the universe, I no longer need to carry a gun.

All of me is beautiful, even the ugly, stupid and disgusting parts.

I am at one with my duality.

Blessed are the flexible, for they can tie themselves into knots.

Only a lack of imagination saves me from immobilising myself with imaginary fears.

I honour and express all facets of my being, regardless of state and local laws.

Today I will gladly share my experience and advice with all who care to hear it, for there are no sweeter words than 'I told you so!

False hope is better than no hope at all.

A good scapegoat is almost as good as a solution.

Why should I waste my time reliving the past when I can spend it worrying about the future?

The complete lack of evidence is the surest sign that the conspiracy is working.

I am learning that criticism is not nearly as effective as sabotage.

Becoming aware of my character defects leads me naturally to the next step of blaming my parents.

To have a successful relationship I must learn to make it look like I'm giving about as much as I'm getting.

I am willing to make the mistakes if someone else is willing to learn from them.

All of the evil that I speak, hear, and see are pleasurable to me.

When counting my blessings, I count backwards from one.

They no longer allow me into the confessional.

When I am here I wish I was there... and I am.

Seminars for Females

Elementary Map Reading

Crying and Law Enforcement

Advanced Mathematics Seminar: Programming Your VCR

You CAN Go Shopping for Less Than Four Hours

Gaining Two Kilos v. the End of the World: A Study in Contrast

The Seven-Outfit Week

Telephone Translations (formerly titled 'Me Too' Equals 'I Love You')

How to Earn Your Own Money

Gift-giving Fundamentals (formerly titled Fabric Bad, Electronics Good)

Putting the Seat Down by Yourself: Potential Energy is on Your Side

What Goes Around Comes Around: Why His Credit Card is Not a Toy

Commitment Schmittment (formerly titled Wedlock Schmedlock)

To Honour and Obey: Remembering the Small Print Above 'I Do'

Why Your Mother Is Unwelcome in the House

Seminars for Males

Combating Stupidity

You, Too, Can Do Housework

PMS: Learn When to Keep Your Mouth Shut

How to Fill an Ice Tray

Understanding the Female Response to Your Coming in Drunk at Four in the Morning

Parenting: No, It Doesn't End With Conception

Get a Life: Learn to Cook

Understanding Your Financial Incompetence

You: the Weaker Sex

Reasons to Give Flowers

Why It Is Unacceptable to Relieve Yourself Anywhere but the Bathroom

You Can Fall Asleep Without 'It' If You Really Try

How to Put the Toilet Lid Down (formerly titled No, It's Not a Bidet)

'The Weekend' and 'Sports' are Not Synonyms

Give Me a Break: Why We Know Your Excuses are Bull

The Remote Control: Overcoming Your Dependency

Helpful Postural Hints for Couch Potatoes

Mothers-in-law: They Are People Too

Male Bonding: Leaving Your Friends at Home

You, Too, Can Be a Designated Driver

Changing Your Underwear: It Really Works

The Attainable Goal: Omitting 'Tits' From Your Vocabulary

Fluffing the Blankets After Flatulence is Really Not Necessary

Training Courses Now Available to Women

Silence, the Final Frontier: Where No Woman Has Gone Before

The Undiscovered Side of Banking: Making Deposits

Bathroom Etiquette I: Men Need Space in the Bathroom Cabinet Too

Bathroom Etiquette II: Get Your Own Razor

Parties: Going Without New Outfits

Communication Skills I: Tears – The Last Resort, Not the First

Communication Skills II: Thinking Before Speaking

Communication Skills III: Getting What You Want Without Nagging

Introduction to Parking

Advanced Parking 101: Attempting the Parallel Park

Advanced Parking 201: Attempting the Parallel Park Without Guidance From Passers-by

Water Retention: Fact or Fat

Cooking I: Bringing Back Bacon, Eggs and Butter

Cooking II: Bran and Tofu Are Not for Human Consumption

Cooking III: How Not to Inflict Your Diets on Other People

Compliments: Accepting Them Gracefully

PMS: Your Problem... Not His

Dancing: Why Men Don't Like To

Classic Clothing: Wearing Outfits You Already Have in Your Wardrobe

Household Dust: A Harmless Natural Occurrence Only Women Notice

Integrating Your Laundry: Washing It All Together

~~~~~~~~

An optimist thinks that this is the best possible world.

The Five Stages of Drunkenness

Stage 1 – Smart

This is when you suddenly become an expert on every subject in the known universe. You know everything and want to pass on your knowledge to anyone who will listen. At this stage you are always *right*. And of course the person you are talking to is very *wrong*. It makes for an interesting argument when both parties are *smart*.

Stage 2 – Good looking

This is when you realise that you are the *best-looking* person in the entire bar and that people fancy you. You can go up to a perfect stranger knowing they all adore the way you look. Bear in mind that you are still *smart*, so you can talk to this person about any subject under the sun.

Stage 3 – Rich

This is when you suddenly become the richest person in the world. You can buy drinks for the entire bar because you have an armoured truck full of money parked behind the bar. You can also make bets at this stage, because of course, you are still *smart*, so naturally you will win all your bets. It doesn't matter how much you bet because you are *rich*.

Stage 4 – Bulletproof

You are now ready to pick fights with anyone and everyone especially those with whom you have been betting or arguing. This is because nothing can hurt you. At this point you can also go up to the partners of the people you fancy and challenge them to a battle of wits or money. You have no fear of losing this battle because not only are you *smart*, you are *rich* and hell, you're *better looking* than they are anyway!

Stage 5 – Invisible

This is the Final Stage of Drunkenness. At this point you can do anything because *no one can see you*. You dance on a table to impress the people you fancy because the rest of the people in the room cannot see you. You are also invisible to the person who wants to fight you. You can walk through the street singing at the top of your lungs because no one can see or hear you and because you're still *smart*, you know all the words.

~~~~~~~

I have kleptomania, but when it gets bad, I take something for it.

~~~~~~~

Even if you are on the right track, you'll get run over if you just sit there.

Baby Talk

Amnesia: A condition that enables a woman who has gone through labour to do it again.

Family planning: The art of spacing your children the proper distance apart to keep you on the edge of financial disaster.

Feedback: The inevitable result when the baby doesn't appreciate the strained carrots.

Full name: What you call your child when you're mad at him or her.

Grandparents: People who think your children are wonderful even though they're sure you're not raising them right.

Hearsay: What toddlers do when anyone mutters a dirty word.

Impregnable: A woman whose memory of labour is still vivid.

Independent: What we want our children to be as long as they do everything we say.

Ow: The first word spoken by children with older siblings.

Prenatal: When your life was still somewhat your own.

Puddle: A small body of water that draws other small bodies wearing dry shoes into it.

Show-off: A child who is more talented than yours.

Sterilise: What you do to your first baby's dummy by boiling it and to your last baby's dummy by blowing on it.

Top bunk: Where you should never put a child wearing Superman pyjamas.

Two-minute warning: When the baby's face turns red and she begins to make those familiar grunting noises.

I've Learned...

I've learned that you cannot make someone love you. All you can do is stalk them and hope they panic and give in.

I've learned that no matter how much I care, some people are just pricks.

I've learned that it takes years to build up trust, and only suspicion, not proof, to destroy it.

I've learned that it's not what you have in your life that counts but how much you have in your bank accounts.

I've learned that you can get by on charm for about 15 minutes. After that, you'd better have a big dick or huge tits.

I've learned that you shouldn't compare yourself to others – they are more stuffed up than you think.

I've learned that you can keep puking long after you think you're finished.

I've learned that regardless of how hot and steamy a relationship is at first, the passion fades, and there had better be a lot of money to take its place.

I've learned that money is a great substitute for character.

I've learned that sometimes the people you expect to kick you when you're down will be the ones who do.

I've learned that we don't have to ditch bad friends because their dysfunction makes us feel better about ourselves.

I've learned that no matter how you try to protect your children, they will eventually get arrested and end up in the local paper.

I've learned that overzealous customs agents can change your life in a matter of hours.

I've learned that the people you care most about in life are taken from you too soon. And all the less important ones just never go away.

~~~~~~~

I still miss my ex-husband, but my aim is improving.

Daily Exercises for the Non-Athletic

Calories can be burned by the hundreds by engaging in strenuous activities that do not require physical exercise.

Exercise	Calories/hr
Beating around the bush	75
Jumping to conclusions	100
Climbing the walls	150
Swallowing your pride	50
Passing the buck	25
Throwing your weight around (depending on your weight)	50-300
Dragging your heels	100
Pushing your luck	250
Making mountains out of molehills	500
Hitting the nail on the head	50
Wading through paperwork	300
Bending over backwards	75
Jumping on the bandwagon	200
Balancing the books	25
Running around in circles	350

Blowing your own trumpet	25
Climbing the ladder of success	750
Adding fuel to the fire	160
Wrapping it up at the day's end	12
Opening a can of worms	50
Putting your foot in your mouth	300
Starting the ball rolling	90
Going over the edge	25
Picking up the pieces after	350

Bumperstickers, Witticisms, One-Liners...

The sex was so good that even the neighbours had a cigarette.

If you smoke after sex, you're doing it too fast.

I don't suffer from insanity, I enjoy every minute of it.

If ignorance is bliss, you must be orgasmic.

Good girls get fat, bad girls get eaten.

The more people I meet, the more I like my dog.

Some people are alive only because it's illegal to kill them.

A bartender is just a pharmacist with a limited inventory.

I used to have a handle on life, but it broke.

Don't take life too seriously. You won't get out alive.

WANTED: Meaningful overnight relationship.

If you can read this, I've lost my trailer.

You're just jealous because the voices only talk to me.

I got a gun for my wife. Best trade I've ever made.

So you're a feminist... isn't that cute!

Jesus may love you, but he won't respect you in the morning.

I don't care, I don't have to.

Beauty is in the eye of the beer holder.

Earth is the insane asylum for the universe.

To all you virgins, thanks for nothing.

Horn broken, watch for finger.

All men are idiots... I married their king.

The more you complain, the longer God lets you live.

Earth first...we'll mine the other planets later.

Please Mr Bank Manager, how can I be overdrawn, I still have cheques!

If at first you do succeed, please try not to look astonished.

Work is for people who don't know how to fish.

While hard work certainly has a future payoff, laziness pays off now.

I'm just driving this way to piss you off.

Jesus paid for our sins... now let's get our money's worth.

Reality is a crutch for people who can't handle drugs.

Missing your cat? Try looking under my tyres.

Out of my mind. Back in five minutes.

I want to be like Barbie – that bitch has everything.

Snatch a kiss, or vice versa.

This would be really funny if it wasn't happening to me.

I get enough exercise pushing my luck.

If you don't like the news, go out and make your own.

Guns don't kill people... but they sure make it easy.

I want to die peacefully in my sleep like my grandpa... not screaming and yelling like the passengers in his car.

Ask me about microwaving cats for fun and profit.

I said 'no' to drugs, but they just wouldn't listen.

If we aren't supposed to eat animals, why are they made of meat?

Friends help you move. Real friends help you move bodies.

Sex on television can't hurt you... unless you fall off.

Honk if you do what car bumper stickers tell you to do.

Stress Management

Picture yourself near a stream. Birds are softly chirping in the crisp, cool mountain air.
Nothing can bother you here. No one knows this secret place. You are in total seclusion from that place called 'the world'. The soothing sound of a gentle waterfall fills the air with a cascade of serenity. The water is so clear... you can easily make out the face of the person whose head you're holding under the water. There now... feeling better?

A Woman's Ultimate Fantasy

Ask any man, and he will tell you that any woman's ultimate fantasy is to have two men at once. While this has been verified by a recent sociological study, it appears that most men do not realise that in this fantasy... one man is cooking and the other is cleaning.

Paycheque Guide

The following helpful guide has been prepared to help our employees better understand their paycheques:

Item	Amount
Gross pay	$1,222.02
Income tax	$244.40
Outgoing tax	$45.21
State tax	$11.61
Interstate tax	$61.10
Regional tax	$6.11
City tax	$12.22
Rural tax	$4.44
Back tax	$1.11
Front tax	$1.16
Side tax	$1.61
Up tax	$2.22
Tic-Tacs	$1.98
Thumbtacks	$3.93

Carpet tacks	$0.98
Stadium tax	$0.69
Flat tax	$8.32
Corporate tax	$2.60
Parking fee	$5.00
Life insurance	$5.85
Health insurance	$16.23
Dental insurance	$4.50
Mental insurance	$4.33
Reassurance	$0.11
Disability	$2.50
Ability	$0.25
Liability	$3.41
Unreliability	$10.99
Coffee	$6.85
Coffee cups	$66.51
Floor rental	$16.85
Chair rental	$0.32
Desk rental	$4.32
Union dues	$5.85
Union don'ts	$3.77
Cash advances	$0.69
Cash retreats	$121.35
Overtime	$1.26
Undertime	$54.83
Eastern time	$9.00
Central time	$8.00
Mountain time	$7.00
Pacific time	$6.00

Time out	$12.21
Oxygen	$10.02
Water	$16.54
Heat	$51.42
Cool air	$26.83
Hot air	$20.00
Miscellaneous	$113.29
Sundry	$12.09
Various	$8.01
Net Take Home Pay	**$0.02**

Thank you for your loyalty to our company. We are here to provide a positive employment experience. All questions, comments, concerns, complaints, frustrations, irritations, aggravations, insinuations, allegations, accusations, contemplations, consternations, or input should be directed elsewhere. Have a nice week.

Intelligence

All babies start out with the same number of raw cells which, over nine months, develop into a complete female baby. The problem occurs when cells are instructed by the little chromosomes to make a male baby instead. Because there are only so many cells to go around, the cell necessary to develop a male's reproductive organs have to come from cells already assigned elsewhere in the female.

Recent tests have shown that these cells are re-moved from the communications centre of the brain, migrate lower in the body and develop into male sexual organs. If you visualise a normal brain to be similar to a full deck of cards, this means that males are born a few cards short, so to speak, and some of their cards are in their shorts.

This difference between the male and female brain manifests itself in various ways. Little girls will tend to play things like house or learn to read. Little boys, however, will tend to do things like placing a bucket over their heads and running into walls. Little girls will think about doing things before taking any action. Little boys will just punch or kick something and will look surprised if someone asks them why they just punched their little brother who was half asleep and looking the other way.

This basic cognitive difference continues to grow until puberty, when the hormones kick into action and the trouble really begins. After puberty, not only the sizes of the male and female brains differ, but the centre of thought also differs. Women think with their heads. Male thoughts often originate lower in their bodies where their ex-brain cells reside.

Of course, the size of this problem varies from man to man. In some men only a small number of brain cells migrate and they are left with nearly full mental capacity but they tend to be rather dull, sexually speaking. Such men are known in medical terms as 'engineers'. Other men suffer larger brain cell relocation. These men are medically referred to as 'lawyers'. A small number of men suffer massive brain cell migration to their groins. These men are usually referred to as ... 'prime minister'.

You Know You're Over the Hill When...

You find yourself beginning to like accordion music.

Lawn care has become a big highlight of your life.

Your undies creep up on you... and you enjoy it.

You tune into the easy listening station... on purpose.

You discover that your measurements are now small, medium and large... in that order.

You keep repeating yourself.

You start videotaping daytime game shows.

At cafeterias, you complain that the jelly is too tough.

Your new easy chair has more options than your car.

When you do the 'Hokey Pokey' you put your left hip out... and it stays out.

One of the throw pillows on your bed is a hot water bottle.

Conversations with people your own age often turn into 'duelling ailments.'

You keep repeating yourself.

It takes a couple of tries to get over a speed bump.

You're on a TV game show and you decide to risk it all and go for the rocker.

You begin every other sentence with, 'Nowadays...'

You run out of breath walking *down* a flight of stairs.

You look both ways before crossing a room.

You come to the conclusion that your worst enemy is gravity.

It takes you all night to do what you used to do all night.

You go to a garden party and you're mainly interested in the garden.

You find your mouth making promises your body can't keep.

At parties you attend, 'regularity' is considered the topic of choice.

You start beating everyone else at trivia games.

You frequently find yourself telling people what a loaf of bread *used* to cost.

Your back goes out more than you do.

You keep repeating yourself.

Your childhood toys are now in a museum.

The clothes you've put away until they come back in style... come back in style.

All of your favourite movies are now revised in colour.

The car that you bought brand new is now a very valuable antique.

You keep repeating yourself.

You find this list tasteless and insensitive.

You Might Be a Bachelor If...

You can clean engine parts in the bathtub without someone yelling at you.

You amuse yourself by lobbing beer cans so that they bounce off the wall before hitting aforementioned bin.

It takes you 10 minutes every six months to buy new clothes (Let's see, I'm out of jeans, white T-shirts, black T-shirts, and socks...)

You don't feel compelled to wear underwear unless you have a date that night.

Your car gets waxed more often than the toilet gets cleaned.

You turn your socks and underwear inside out so you can wear them twice as long.

You have the pizza place on the speed dial.

Instead of cleaning for guests, you just keep the lights low.

Paper towels double as dishes.

Beer is the freshest item in the fridge.

Beer is the only item in the fridge.

You never listen to your messages when a female is around.

Your entire house is trashed except for your TV and stereo, which are lovingly polished every day.

If anything needs to be cooked longer than five minutes, it is a waste of time.

The last time you cleaned the house was when you moved in.

A dress shirt is 'fine' if it only has one or two wrinkles in it.

You don't feel guilty about leaving the toilet seat **up.**

How to Take a Shower

How to Shower Like a Woman

Take off clothing and place it in sectioned laundry hamper according to whites and coloureds.

Walk to bathroom wearing long dressing gown. If you see your boyfriend/husband along the way, cover up any exposed flesh and rush to the bathroom.

Look at your womanly physique in the mirror and stick out your gut so that you can complain and whine even more about how you're getting fat.

Get in the shower. Look for facecloth, arm-cloth, long loofah, wide loofah and pumice stone.

Wash your hair once with cucumber shampoo with 83 added vitamins.

Wash your hair again with cucumber shampoo with 83 added vitamins.

Condition your hair with cucumber conditioner enhanced with natural crocus oil. Leave on hair for 15 minutes.

Wash your face with crushed apricot facial scrub for 10 minutes until red raw.

Wash entire rest of body with gingernut body wash.

Rinse conditioner from hair. (This takes at least 15 minutes as you must make sure that it has all come off.)

Shave armpits and legs. Consider shaving bikini area but decide to get it waxed instead.

Scream loudly when your boyfriend/husband flushes the toilet and you lose the water pressure.

Turn off shower.

Squeegee off all wet surfaces in shower. Spray mould spots.

Get out of shower. Dry with towel the size of a small African country. Wrap hair in super-absorbent second towel.

Check entire body for the remotest sign of a zit.

Attack with nails/tweezers if found.

Return to bedroom wearing long dressing gown and towel on head.

If you see your boyfriend/husband along the way, cover up any exposed flesh and then rush to bedroom to spend at least an hour-and-a-half getting dressed.

How to Shower Like a Man

Take off clothes while sitting on the edge of the bed and leave them in a pile.

Walk naked to the bathroom. If you see your girlfriend/wife along the way, flash her, making the 'woo, woo' sound.

Look at your manly physique in the mirror and suck in your gut and scratch yourself.

Get in the shower.

Don't bother to look for a washcloth. (You don't use one.)

Wash your face.

Wash your armpits.

Crack up at how loud your fart sounds in the shower.

Wash your privates and surrounding area.

Wash your arse, leaving hair on the soap bar.

Shampoo your hair. (Do not use conditioner.)

Make a shampoo mohawk.

Pull back shower curtain and look at yourself in the mirror.

Pee (in the shower).

Rinse off and get out of the shower. Fail to notice water on the floor because you left the curtain hanging out of the tub when you checked your mohawk.

Partially dry off.

Look at yourself in the mirror, flex muscles. Admire willy size.

Leave shower curtain open and wet bath mat on the floor.

Leave bathroom fan and light on.

Return to the bedroom with towel around your waist. If you pass your girlfriend/wife, pull off the towel, go 'Yeah baby' and thrust your pelvis at her.

Throw wet towel on the bed. Take two minutes to get dressed.

You Know It's Going to Be a Bad Day When...

Your twin forgets your birthday.

You wake up face down on the pavement.

You see a 60 Minutes news team waiting in your outer office.

Your birthday cake collapses from the weight of the candles.

You want to put on the clothes you wore home from the party, and there aren't any.

You turn on the TV news and they're displaying emergency routes out of your city.

Your doctor tells you, 'Well, I have bad news and good news...'

You open the paper and find your picture under a caption that reads: 'Wanted: Dead or Alive'.

Your ex-lover calls and tells you he/she has six days to live, and that you'd better get yourself tested.

You have an appointment in 10 minutes and you just woke up.

You wake up at work naked in front of your co-workers.

BMW Auto Terminology

Indicators – Die Blinkenleiten Tickentocken

Speedometer – Der Egobooster

Learner – Die Twaten mit Elplatten

Windscreen wiper – Die Flippenflappenschittenspredden

Breathalyser – Die Puffintem fur Pistenarsen

Fog warning – Die Puttenfutdownen Fukit

Near accident – Der Bleepin neer Schittenselfen

Cyclist – Pedalpushen pilloken

Rear view mirror – Der Yokhunter Tooklosen

Statements to Avoid During a Job Interview

'You could do worse.'

'I'll work so hard you won't even know I'm here.'

'I'll need all my paid annual leave up front so I'll be rested when I start.'

'You can't turn me down because I smell bad. You have to have a reason.'

'That big thing growing on my face isn't my fault.'

'I don't do drugs at work any more. I swear.'

'I can go all day without peeing once.'

'I won't sue you when you fire me.'

'My arrest record is all a bunch of lies.'

'The sticky stuff on my hands isn't what you think.'

'I was a sniper in the army.'

'I can make explosives from Windex, white-out, and photocopier toner.'

'The sticky stuff on my sleeve isn't what you think.'

'You don't have the BALLS to hire someone like me!'

'If you hire me I will show up. That's all I can promise for sure, but maybe it will be better than that and I will sure try.'

'When do we eat?'

'Don't go checking into my record, but if you do, she swore she was 18.'

'I don't hear the voices anymore. Do not. Do not. Do not. SHUT UP!'

'If you give me a job you're okay, but if you don't you suck.'

'I don't *do* applications.'

'If I work here I'll wear the stupid uniform as long as I can wear any kind of underwear I want.'

'That sticky stuff in my chair isn't what you think.'

'I won't have to do anything, will I?'

'Can I bring my goat to the company day-care centre?'

'I collect guns. You probably want to tell me that I got the job now, right?'

'I'm not what? Oh yeah? Well here's what you can do with your friggin' job...'

The Rules of Indoor Badminton

In order to score, a player must land his cock in his opponent's court.

Players may only handle the cock before serving or after scoring.

If a player does not get the cock into his opponent's court for any reason then he does not score and cannot try again until he has service again.

Damaged cocks should not be used as this can cause irritation to the court surface.

Rubber covers are advised for safety, as they are about 99% less likely to damage the court.

Courts with worn or damaged patches should not be used for at least two weeks.

If while playing the cock lands out of the court the players should clean up and carry on with the game unless they are too tired.

The type of cock and size of court should not affect players' enjoyment of the game.

Large courts are not advisable for play as generally they have been overused in the past.

If the opponent is not ready to receive a service for any reason, play should be suspended.

To aid play the players should keep an eye on the cock and court at all times.

To increase service length the server can use a different type of racquet. This is more likely to stimulate interesting play.

If the game does not involve mixed singles then the area of play should be changed.

Inspirational Posters

Rome did not create a great empire by having meetings; they did it by killing all those who opposed them.

If you can stay calm, while all around you is chaos... then you probably haven't completely understood the seriousness of the situation.

Doing a job right the first time gets the job done.

Doing the job wrong 14 times gives you job security.

Artificial Intelligence is no match for Natural Stupidity.

A person who smiles in the face of adversity... probably has a scapegoat.

If at first you don't succeed, try management.

Never put off until tomorrow what you can avoid altogether.

Teamwork... means never having to take all the blame yourself.

The beatings will continue until morale improves.

Never underestimate the power of very stupid people in large groups.

We waste time, so you don't have to.

Hang in there; retirement is only 30 years away!

Go the extra mile. It makes your boss look like an incompetent slacker.

A snooze button is a poor substitute for no alarm clock at all.

When the going gets tough, the tough take a coffee break.

Indecision is the key to flexibility.

Succeed in spite of management.

Aim low, reach your goals, and you will avoid disappointment.

~~~~~~~

Never replicate a successful experiment.

~~~~~~~

Make failure your teacher, not your undertaker.

Letters of Recommendation

Have to write a letter of recommendation for that fired employee? Here are a few suggested phrases:

For the chronically absent:
'A man like him is hard to find.'
'It seemed her career was just taking off.'

For the office drunk:
'I feel his real talent is wasted here.'
'We generally found him loaded with work to do.'
'Every hour with him was a happy hour.'

For an employee with no ambition:
'He could not care less about the number of hours he had to put in.'
'You would indeed be fortunate to get this person to work for you.'

For an employee who is so unproductive that the job is better left unfilled:
'I can assure you that no person would be better for the job.'

For an employee who is not worth further consideration as a job candidate:
'I would urge you to waste no time in making this candidate an offer of employment.'
'All in all, I cannot say enough good things about this candidate or recommend him too highly.'

For a stupid employee:
'There is nothing you can teach a man like him.'
'I most enthusiastically recommend this candidate with no qualifications whatsoever.'

For a dishonest employee:
'Her true ability was deceiving.'
'He's an unbelievable worker.'

Have to read a letter of recommendation? Here are a few translations:

'A keen analyst.'
Thoroughly confused.

'Accepts new job assignments willingly.'
Never finishes a job.

'Active socially.'
Drinks heavily.

'Alert to company developments.'
An office gossip.

'Approaches difficult problems with logic.'
Finds someone else to do the job.

'Bridge builder.'
Likes to compromise.

'Character above reproach.'
Still one step ahead of the law.

'Charismatic.'
No interest in any opinion but his own.

'Competent.'
Is still able to get work done if supervisor helps.

'Conscientious and careful.'
Scared.

'Consults with co-workers often.'
Indecisive, confused, and clueless.

'Consults with supervisor often.'
Pain in the arse.

'Delegates responsibility effectively.'
Passes the buck well.

'Demonstrates qualities of leadership.'
Has a loud voice.

'Deserves promotion.'
Create new title to make him/her feel appreciated.

'Displays excellent intuitive judgement.'
Knows when to disappear.

'Displays great dexterity and agility.'
Dodges and evades superiors well.

'Enjoys job.'
Needs more to do.

'Excels in sustaining concentration but avoids confrontations.'
Ignores everyone.

'Excels in the effective application of skills.'
Makes a good cup of coffee.

'Exceptionally well qualified.'
Has committed no major blunders to date.

'Expresses self well.'
Can string two sentences together.

'Gets along extremely well with superiors and subordinates alike.'
A coward.

'Happy.'
Paid too much.

'Hard worker.'
Usually does it the hard way.

'Identifies major management problems.'
Complains a lot.

'Indifferent to instruction.'
Knows more than superiors.

'Is well informed.'
Knows all office gossip and where all the skeletons are kept.

'Inspires the cooperation of others.'
Gets everyone else to do the work.

'Is unusually loyal.'
Wanted by no one else.

'Judgement is usually sound.'
Lucky.

'Keen sense of humour.'
Knows lots of dirty jokes.

'Keeps informed on business issues.'
Subscribes to Playboy *and* National Enquirer.

'Listens well.'
Has no ideas of his own.

'Maintains a high degree of participation.'
Comes to work on time.

'Maintains professional attitude.'
A snob.

'Meticulous in attention to detail.'
A nitpicker.

'Mover and shaker.'
Favours steamroller tactics without regard for other people's opinions.

'Not a desk person.'
Did not go to university.

'Uses all available resources.'
Takes office supplies home for personal use.

'Quick thinking.'
Offers plausible excuses for errors.

'Should go far.'
Please.

'Spends extra hours on the job.'
Miserable home life.

'Straightforward.'
Blunt and insensitive.

'Strong adherence to principles.'
Stubborn.

'Tactful in dealing with superiors.'
Knows when to keep mouth shut.

'Takes utmost advantage of every opportunity to progress.'
Buys drinks for superiors.

'Takes pride in work.'
Conceited.

'Uses time effectively.'
Clock watcher.

'Very creative.'
Finds 22 reasons to do anything except original work.

'Will go far.'
Relative of management.

'Willing to take calculated risks.'
Doesn't mind spending someone else's money.

~~~~~~~~~

It's easier to fight for one's principles than to live up to them.

Marriage One-liners

Marriage is not a word. It is a sentence (a life sentence!).

Marriage is very much like a violin; after the sweet music is over, the strings are attached.

Marriage is love. Love is blind. Therefore, marriage is an institution for the blind.

Marriage is a thing that puts a ring on a woman's finger and two under the man's eyes.

Marriage certificate is just another word for a work permit.

Married life is full of excitement and frustration. In the first year of marriage, the man speaks and the woman listens. In the second year, the woman speaks and the man listens. In the third year, they both speak and the neighbours listen.

Getting married is very much like going to the restaurant with friends. You order what you want, and when you see what the other fellow has, you wish you had ordered that.

It's true that all men are born free and equal, but some of them get married!

A happy marriage is a matter of giving and taking; the husband gives and the wife takes.

Son: How much does it cost to get married, Dad?
Father: I don't know son, I'm still paying for it.

Son: Dad, I heard that in ancient China, a man doesn't know his wife until he marries. Is it true?
Father: That happens everywhere, son, EVERYWHERE!

There was a man who said, 'I never knew what happiness was until I got married... and then it was too late!'

Love is one long sweet dream, and marriage is the alarm clock.

They say when a man holds a woman's hand before marriage, it is love; after marriage, it is self-defence.

When a newly married man looks happy, we know why. But when a man who has been married for 10 years looks happy, we wonder why.

What the Doctor Really Means

Doctor says: 'This should be taken care of right away.'
Doctor means: I'd planned a trip to Hawaii next month but this is so easy and profitable that I want to fix it before it cures itself.

Doctor says: 'Welllllll, what have we here...'
Doctor means: Since I haven't the foggiest notion of what it is, I'm hoping you will give me a bit of a clue.

Doctor says: 'We'll see.'
Doctor means: First I have to check my malpractice insurance.

Doctor says: 'Let me check your medical history.'
Doctor means: I want to see if you've paid your last bill before spending any more time with you.

Doctor says: 'Why don't we make another appointment later in the week.'
Doctor means: I'm playing golf this afternoon, and this a waste of time. Or, I need the money, so I'm charging you for another office visit.

Doctor says: 'I really can't recommend seeing a chiropractor.'
Doctor means: I hate those guys mooching in on our fees.

Doctor says: 'We have some good news and some bad news.'
Doctor means: The good news is he's going to buy that new BMW, and the bad news is you're going to pay for it.

Doctor says: 'Let's see how it develops.'
Doctor means: Maybe in a few days it will grow into something that can be cured.

Doctor says: 'Let me schedule you for some tests.'
Doctor means: I have a 40% interest in the lab.

Doctor says: 'How are we today?'
Doctor means: I feel great. You, on the other hand, look like hell.

Doctor says: 'I'd like to prescribe a new drug.'
Doctor means: I'm writing a paper and would like to use you as a guinea pig.

Doctor says: 'If it doesn't clear up in a week, give me a call.'
Doctor means: I don't know what the hell it is. Maybe it will go away by itself.

Doctor says: 'That's quite a nasty-looking wound.'
Doctor means: I think I'm going to throw up.

Doctor says: 'This may sting a little.'
Doctor means: Last week two patients bit through their tongues.

Doctor says: 'This should fix you up.'
Doctor means: The drug salesman guaranteed that it kills all symptoms.

Doctor says: 'Everything seems to be normal.'
Doctor means: I guess I can't buy that new beach house after all.

Doctor says: 'I'd like to run some more tests.'
Doctor means: I can't figure out what's wrong. Maybe the kid in the lab can solve this one.

Doctor says: 'Do you suppose all of this stress could be affecting your nerves?'
Doctor means: He thinks you are crazy and is hoping to find a psychiatrist who will split fees.

What is the Definition of...

Amnesia... What did you just ask me?

Apathy... I don't care.

Bigotry... I'm not going to tell someone like you.

Damnation... Go to hell!

Dyslexia... Beeing sackwards.

Egotistical... I'm the best person to answer that question.

Flatulent... That question really stinks!

Hostility... If you ask me just one more question, I'll kill you!

Ignorance... I don't know.

Indifference... It doesn't matter.

Influenza... You've got to be sick to ask me that question.

Insomnia... I stayed awake all last night thinking of the answer.

Irreverent… I swear to God, you ask too many questions!

Masturbation… Your father can handle that question.

Narcissism… Before I answer, tell me, don't I look great?

Over-protective… I don't know if you're ready for the answer.

Paranoid… You probably think I don't know the answer, don't you?

Procrastination… I'll tell you tomorrow.

Repetitive… I already told you the answer once before.

Self-centred… Well, I know the answer, that's all that matters.

Suspicious… Why are you asking me all these questions?

~~~~~~~~

It hurts to be on the cutting edge.

~~~~~~~~

I don't get even, I get odder.

As Effective As...

A one-legged man in an arse-kicking contest.

Milk shoes.

A nuclear-powered computer-controlled inter-continental ballistic duck.

A flammable fire extinguisher.

A glass cricket bat.

A blind lifeguard.

Wooden soap.

A knitted light bulb.

An invisible traffic light.

Plasticine wire cutters.

A neon pink secret door.

A lead balloon.

A water hat.

A steel-reinforced concrete sail.

A silent telephone.

A tap-dancing microprocessor-controlled portrait of a bowl of soup.

A waterproof tea bag.

A liquorice suspension bridge.

Soap false teeth.

Ice-cream saucepans.

A soluble drain pipe.

A cubic ball-bearing.

An inflatable dartboard.

A soluble lifeboat.

A glass hammer.

And a packet of rubber nails.

A see-through mirror.

Revolving basement restaurant.

Objective journalism.

Braille speedometers.

A screen door on a submarine.

An ejector seat in a helicopter.

A sodium submarine.

Tits on a bull.

A condom with a hole in it.

A box of matches in the desert.

~~~~~~~~~

In just two days, tomorrow will be yesterday.

So Many Lies, So Little Time

Lies about Love

Everyone does this, it's perfectly normal.

It's dangerous to your health to get excited and then stop.

I'll stop as soon as you say.

I'll tell her/him tonight.

Well, the clinic said I was clear!

Nobody can hear us.

I'll never put myself through this again.

Men's Lies

Sex isn't everything.

It's not your fault.

It's too late.

I read an article today.

I'm allergic to rubber.

We'll try again when we wake up.

It has a mind of its own.

This has never happened before.

Party Lies

I'm not going to drink too much tonight.

They'll all be wearing jeans.

There are no bones in this fish.

The neighbours are very tolerant.

Just half a glass, thanks.

He doesn't normally act like this when he's been drinking.

It's no trouble if you stay the night.

Salesman Lies

You won't see this anywhere else.

This sort of thing never goes out of fashion.

Bring it back if you don't like it.

This is a never-to-be-repeated offer!

Unbelievably low prices.

It's the last one in stock.

You'll have no trouble with it.

Drivers Stopped by the Law Lies

I was just going the speed limit.

I only had one.

What stop sign?

The light was green when I started through the intersection.

He came from nowhere when I changed lanes.

Officer, I can walk without any assistance.

Computer Lies

If you have any problems, just call us.

What you see on the screen, you get on paper.

They don't make those chips any more.

If kids use them, so can adults.

Oh yeah, it's compatible with everything.

You won't need any special training.

There's no harm in trying – nothing can go wrong.

The manual explains everything.

The Parachute Paradigm

You are one of two people on a malfunctioning aeroplane with only one parachute.

Pessimist: you refuse the parachute because you might die in the jump anyway.

Optimist: you refuse the parachute because people have survived jumps just like this before.

Procrastinator: you play a game of Monopoly for the parachute.

Bureaucrat: you order the other person to conduct a feasibility study on parachute use in multi-engine aircraft under code red conditions.

Lawyer: you charge one parachute for helping the other person sue the airline.

Doctor: you tell the other person you need to run more tests, then take the parachute in order to make your next appointment.

Sales executive: you sell the other person the parachute at top retail rates and get the names of their friends and relatives who might like one too.

Advertiser: you strip-tease while singing that what the other person needs is a neon parachute with computer altimeter for only $39.99.

Engineer: you make the other person another parachute out of aisle curtains and dental floss.

Scientist: you give the other person the parachute and ask them to send you a report on how well it worked.

Mathematician: you refuse to accept the parachute without proof that it will work in all cases.

Philosopher: you ask how the other person knows the parachute actually exists.

English expert: you explicate simile and metaphor in the parachute instructions.

Comparative literature theorist: you read the parachute instructions in all four languages.

Computer scientist: you design a machine capable of operating a parachute as well as a human being could.

Psychoanalyst: you ask the other person what the shape of a parachute reminds them of.

Dramatist: you tie the other person down so they can watch you develop the character of a person stuck on a falling plane without a parachute.

Artist: you hang the parachute on the wall and sign it.

Environmentalist: you refuse to use the parachute unless it is biodegradable.

Economist: you plot a demand curve by asking them, at regular intervals, how much they would pay for a parachute.

Signs of Life

On an executive's desk: Nobody's perfect. I'm the perfect example.

On a politician's desk: Truth is a precious commodity and therefore should be used as sparingly as possible.

On a secretary's desk: Fact-finding beats fault-finding.

At a health insurance office: Get out reliable health insurance. Don't make your doctor perform a walletectomy.

At a mechanic's: An idealist – one who has both feet firmly planted in the air.

In a manager's office: Sometimes silence is the best way to yell.

On an office desk in a large business: They don't dare fire me. I'm always too far behind in my work.

On an office wall: Even moderation ought not to be practised to excess.

On the same office wall: One of the greatest labour-saving devices of today is tomorrow.

Outside an auto muffler shop: No appointment necessary. We hear you coming.

Beside a dentist's office: Patient parking only. All others will be painfully extracted.

Over a barn door: Agriculture is something like farming, only farming is doing it.

In a restaurant: Don't tip the waiters – it upsets them.

In a store: Credit extended to those over 80 if accompanied by their grandparents.

In a science lab: Tragedy is the murder of a beautiful theory by a brutal gang of facts.

On a marriage counsellor's door: Back in an hour. Don't fight.

On a ski slope: Going beyond this point may result in death and/or loss of skiing privileges.

At the entrance to a school administration building: Education will broaden a narrow mind, but there is no known cure for a big head.

In a cemetery: No trespassing. Violators will be haunted.

Murphy's Laws of Work

A pat on the back is only a few centimetres from a kick in the pants.

Don't be irreplaceable. If you can't be replaced, you can't be promoted.

The more crap you put up with, the more crap you are going to get.

You can go anywhere you want if you look serious and carry a clipboard.

Eat one live toad the first thing in the morning and nothing worse will happen to you the rest of the day.

Never ask two questions in a business letter. The reply will discuss the one you are least interested in, and say nothing about the other.

When the bosses talk about improving productivity, they are never talking about themselves.

If at first you don't succeed, try again. Then quit. No use being a damn fool about it.

There will always be beer cans rolling on the floor of your car when the boss asks for a ride home from the office.

Mother said there would be days like this, but she never said there would be so many.

Keep your boss's boss off your boss's back.

Everything can be filed under 'miscellaneous.'

Never delay the ending of a meeting or the beginning of a cocktail hour.

Anyone can do any amount of work provided it isn't the work he is supposed to be doing.

Important letters that contain no errors will develop errors in the mail.

The last person that quit or was fired will be the one held responsible for everything that goes wrong...until the next person quits or is fired.

There is never enough time to do it right the first time, but there is always enough time to do it over.

The more pretentious a corporate name, the smaller the organisation.

If you are good, you will be assigned all the work. If you are really good, you will get out of it.

If it weren't for the last minute, nothing would get done.

At work, the authority of a person is inversely proportional to the number of pens that person is carrying.

When you don't know what to do, walk fast and look worried.

You will always get the greatest recognition for the job you least like.

No one gets sick on Wednesdays.

When confronted by a difficult problem you can solve it more easily by reducing it to the question,

'How would the Lone Ranger handle this?'

The longer the title, the less important the job.

Machines that have broken down will work perfectly when the repairman arrives.

Once a job is fouled up, anything done to improve it makes it worse.

All holidays create problems, except for one's own.

Success is just a matter of luck, just ask any failure.

The first 90% of the project takes 90% of the time; the last 10% takes the other 90% of the time.

It doesn't matter what you do, it only matters what you say you've done and what you're going to do.

After any salary raise, you will have less money at the end of the month than you did before.

People who go to conferences are the ones who shouldn't.

Following the rules will not get the job done.

Getting the job done is no excuse for not following the rules.

Murphy's Laws for Frequent Flyers

No flight ever leaves on time unless you are running late and need the delay to make the flight.

If you are running late for a flight, it will depart from the farthest gate within the terminal.

If you arrive very early for a flight, it inevitably will be delayed.

Flights never leave from Gate #1 at any terminal in the world.

If you must work on your flight, you will experience turbulence as soon as you touch pen to paper.

If you are assigned a middle seat, you can determine who has the seats on the aisle and the window while you are still in the boarding area. Just look for the two largest passengers.

Only passengers seated in window seats ever have to get up to go to the toilet.

The crying baby on board your flight is always seated next to you.

The best-looking woman/man on your flight is never seated next to you.

The less carry-on luggage space available on an aircraft, the more carry-on luggage passengers will bring aboard.

You Know You're Drinking Too Much Coffee When...

You get a speeding ticket when you're parked.

You have a bumper sticker that says: 'Coffee drinkers are good in the sack.'

You answer the door before people knock.

You just completed another scarf and you don't know how to knit.

You grind your coffee beans in your mouth.

You have to watch videos in fast-forward.

You can take a picture of yourself from 10 feet away without using the timer.

You lick your coffeepot clean.

You're the employee of the month at the local coffeehouse and you don't even work there.

The nurse needs a scientific calculator to take your pulse.

Your t-shirt says, 'Decaffeinated coffee is the devil's coffee.'

You're so jittery that people use your hands to blend their margaritas.

You can type 60 words per minute with your feet. Cocaine is a downer.

You've built a miniature city out of little stirrers.

Instant coffee takes too long.

You want to be cremated just so you can spend the rest of eternity in a coffee jar.

You go to sleep just so you can wake up and smell the coffee.

You're offended when people use the word 'brew' to mean beer.

You have a picture of your coffee mug on your coffee mug.

You can outlast the Energiser bunny.

Your lover uses soft lights, romantic music, and a glass of iced coffee to get you in the mood.

You introduce your spouse as your coffee mate.

Your urine stream bores a hole in the toilet.

You have two complete orgasms while brushing your teeth.

You talk so fast your tongue has windburn.

You jog to work and arrive yesterday.

Your farts smell like espresso.

Your eyes are brown... even the white parts.

You personally account for more than 1% of the gross national product of Brazil.

Your espresso smells like farts.

Mosquitoes that bite you can fly through glass.

You bungee jump and go up.

Your coffee breath etches glass.

You think skydiving is just too damned slow.

~~~~~~~~~

I am an escapee of a political correction facility.

Corporate Zodiac

Astrology tells us about people and their future by their time, date and location of birth. The Chinese Zodiac uses the year of a person's birth. Demographics tell us what others like, dislike, who they voted for, as well as what they buy and what they watch on television. The Corporate Zodiac goes a step further: simply by an individual's job title, people can pretty much learn about an employee's hidden personality traits.

Marketing

You are ambitious, yet stupid. You chose a marketing degree to avoid having to study in university, concentrating instead on drinking and socialising – which is pretty much what your job responsibilities are now. Least compatible with sales.

Sales

Laziest of all the Corporate Signs, often referred to as a 'marketer without a degree'. You are also self-centred and paranoid. Unless someone calls you and begs you to take their money, you like to avoid all contact with customers so you can 'concentrate on the big picture'. You seek admiration for your golf game, clothes, car and sex appeal throughout your career.

Customer Service

Bright, cheery, positive, you are a 50-cent taxi ride from taking your own life. As a child very few of you asked your parents for a little cubicle for your room and a headset so you could pretend to play 'Customer Service'. Continually passed over for promotions, your best bet is to sleep with your manager.

Technology

Unable to control anything in your personal life, you are instead content to completely control everything that happens at your workplace. Typically you went to a trade school because you didn't have time for all that 'crap' required in university. Often, even you don't understand what the hell you're saying, but no one else except the engineers knows anyway. It is written that the geeks shall inherit the earth, but the senior managers keep contesting the will.

Engineering

One of only two signs that actually studied in school, it is said that 60% of all the people on the Internet are either engineers, or wish they were. You can be happy with yourself and the latest technology in your field. Your office is typically full of all the latest gadgets, catalogues and half-finished spec sheets.

Accounting

The only other sign that studied in school, you are mostly immune from office politics. You are the most feared person in the organisation; combined with your extreme organisational traits, the majority of your co-workers are convinced that you are completely without feeling or emotion. You are often caught in the bathroom, practising your frown in the mirror.

Human Resources

Ironically, given your access to confidential information, you tend to be the biggest gossip in the company. Possibly the only other person that does less work than marketing, you are unable to return any calls today because you have to get a haircut, have lunch, and mail a letter! Your favourite expression is: 'Now don't say anything, but...'

Mid-level Managers/Department Heads/Team Leaders

Cut-throat and ambitious, but... you are destined to remain at your current job forever unless a senior manager dies or retires. You measure your worth by the number of meetings you can schedule for yourself and the number of subordinates you sleep with. Best suited to marry other middle managers, as everyone in your social circle must be at least a middle manager for appearance's sake.

Senior Managers

You enjoy appearing to be the ultimate authority figure but actually, you are completely spineless, and determined to remain at your current job for the rest of your life, unless the head of your organisation dies or retires. Unable to make a single decision, you tend to measure your worth by the number of mid-level managers you can harass on any given day and ensure that your office is the largest in the building. Best suited to date/marry other senior managers, as everyone in your social circle is a senior manager; besides, no one else would have you anyway.

The Procrastinator's Creed

I believe that if anything is worth doing, it would have been done already.

I shall never move quickly, except to avoid more work or find excuses.

I will never rush into a job without a lifetime of consideration.

I shall meet all of my deadlines at work and at home directly in proportion to the amount of bodily injury I could expect to receive from missing them.

I truly believe that all deadlines are unreasonable regardless of the amount of time given.

I firmly believe that tomorrow holds the possibility for new technologies, astounding discoveries, and a reprieve from my obligations.

If at first I don't succeed, there is always next year. And if not next year, the year after that.

I shall always decide not to decide, unless of course I decide to change my mind.

I shall always begin, start, initiate, take the first step, and/or write the first word, when I get around to it.

The Office Prayer

Grant me the serenity
To accept the things I cannot change,
The courage
To change the things I cannot accept,
And the wisdom
To hide the bodies of those people
I had to kill today because they pissed me off.
And help me to be careful
Of the toes I step on today,
As they may be connected to the arse
That I might have to kiss tomorrow.

10 Reasons Women Date Losers Instead of Nice Guys

It is more fun to complain about them.

Guys who actually like you just aren't challenging or exciting.

When you do date nice guys, they turn into losers anyway, so why not save time and go for the loser in the first place?

You won't get as emotionally attached to a loser, so you'll be more in control.

All the other women want them, so they must be worth having.

Affection means more when it comes from a guy who doesn't normally give it.

They are guaranteed to cheat on you so someone else can endure his lack of lovemaking skills instead.

There is no need to feel guilty for abusing or deceiving them.

Losers will actually tell you when they don't like what you're doing instead of getting mad about it six months later.

You are looking for someone you can't trust, and won't care about too much, who will abuse you mentally and financially, but you don't know any lawyers.

The Dictionary of Dating

Attraction – the act of associating horniness with a particular person.

Birth control – avoiding pregnancy through such tactics as swallowing special pills, inserting a diaphragm, using a condom, dating repulsive men or spending time around children.

Dating – the process of spending huge amounts of money, time, and energy to get better acquainted with a person whom you don't especially like in the present and will learn to like a lot less in the future.

Easy – a term used to describe a woman who has the sexual morals of a man.

Eye contact – a method utilised by a single woman to communicate to a man that she is interested in him. Despite being advised to do so, many woman have difficulty looking a man directly in the eyes, not necessarily due to the shyness, but usually due to the fact that a woman's eyes are not located in her chest.

Friend – a member of the opposite sex in your acquaintance who has some flaw which makes sleeping with him/her totally unappealing.

Frigid – a man's term for a woman who wants to have sex less often than he does, or who requires more foreplay than ripping her jeans off.

Indifference – a woman's feeling towards a man, which is interpreted by the man as 'playing hard to get.'

Interesting – a word a man uses to describe a woman who lets him do all the talking.

Irritating habit – what the endearing little qualities that initially attract two people to each other turn into after a few months together.

Law of relativity – how attractive a given person appears to be is directly proportional to how unattractive your own date is.

Love at first sight – what occurs when two extremely horny, but not entirely choosy people meet.

Nag – a man's term for a woman who wants more to her life with him than just intercourse.

Nymphomaniac – a man's term for a woman who wants to have sex more often than he does.

Prude – a term used to describe a woman who wants to stay a virgin until married.

Sober – condition in which it is almost impossible to fall in love.

~~~~~~~~~

I don't mind going nowhere as long as it's an interesting path.

Similarities Between Men and Dogs

Both take up too much space on the bed.

Both have irrational fears about vacuum cleaning.

Both are threatened by their own kind.

Both like to chew wood.

Both mark their territory.

Both are bad at asking you questions.

Neither tells you what's bothering them.

Both tend to smell riper with age.

The smaller ones tend to be more nervous.

Neither do any dishes.

Neither of them notice when you get your haircut.

Both like dominance games.

Both are suspicious of the postman.

Neither knows how to talk on the telephone.

Neither understands what you see in cats.

~~~~~~~~~

If at first you don't succeed, then skydiving isn't for you.

251

Pick-up Line Rebuttals

Man: I know how to please a woman.
Woman: Then please leave me alone.

Man: I want to give myself to you.
Woman: Sorry, I don't accept cheap gifts.

Man: Your hair colour is fabulous.
Woman: Thank you. It's on aisle three at the super-market down the street.

Man: You look like a dream.
Woman: Go back to sleep.

Man: I can tell that you want me.
Woman: Yes, I want you to leave.

Man: I'd go through anything for you.
Woman: Let's start with your bank account.

Man: May I have the last dance?
Woman: You've just had it.

Man: Your place or mine?
Woman: Both. You go to your place, and I'll go to mine.

Man: Is this seat empty?
Woman: Yes, and this one will be too if you sit down.

Man: Haven't I seen you somewhere before?
Woman: Yeah, that's why I don't go there any more.

Why Does He Always Have To...

Be dressed and ready to go before you are?

Get off the phone in a microsecond if he answers when your mother calls?

Pretend he likes stars like Julia Roberts and Sharon Stone because of their acting ability?

Drive 20 kilometres over the speed limit?

Act as if his razor is priceless and should never be touched?

Toss change, keys, and credit cards on the dresser, no matter how many charming containers you provide?

Hand you the 'lifestyle section' when you ask for part of the paper?

Make elaborate snacks the minute you've finished cleaning the kitchen?

Be such a charmer with your best friend after you've privately told her what a beast he's been all week?

Drink milk from the carton with great gusto?

Not understand the 'toilet-seat thing'?

Assume you will take care of gifts, cards and flowers for his family?

Want you to make a fuss when he does some little household chore unasked?

Say 'I am listening to you' when he's not?

Get lost rather than ask for directions?

Wait until you are dressed and made-up to suggest a quickie?

Wash all the dishes in the sink, but leave the big, dirty pots and pans for you?

Be convinced, no matter what you tell him, bigger is better?

Stand at the refrigerator, shouting, 'Honey, where's the mustard?' when it's right in front of him?

Spend hours measuring and making minute pencil marks on the wall when you ask him to hang up a few framed photos, then plop on the couch for the rest of the weekend with the weariness of a man who's just single-handedly built the railroad?

Take charge of everybody's automatic window buttons in the car?

Say 'I'm starving' the minute you walk in the door?

Revert to the age of two during minor illnesses.

Hit the shower immediately after sex?

Be sent to the store with a detailed shopping list and return with four six-packs and an economy-size bag of home-brand chips?

Constantly ask, 'Where'd I put my keys?' as though you watch his every move?

Complain there's nothing on TV but keep watching (and channel surfing) for the rest of the evening?

Observe that you have a closet full of stuff you never wear just as you're leaving to go clothes shopping?

Leave his shoes in the living room?

Eat the last piece of leftover chicken and stick the Glad-Wrapped empty plate back in the fridge?

Readjust his private parts in front of you as if you're not looking?

Accuse you of having PMS?

Hold an umbrella over you so that the rain invariably drips down your neck?

Tell you to 'Shhh' until the next commercial – even if what you have to say is important?

Facts About Women

Women love to shop. It is the one area of the world where they feel like they're actually in control.

Women especially love a bargain. The question of 'need' is irrelevant, so don't bother pointing it out. Anything on sale is fair game.

Women never have anything to wear. Don't question the racks of clothes in the wardrobe; you 'just don't understand'.

Women need to cry. And they won't do it alone unless they know you can hear them.

Women will always ask questions that have no right answer, in an effort to trap you into feeling guilty.

Women love to talk. Silence intimidates them and they feel a need to fill it, even if they have nothing to say.

Women need to feel like there are people worse off than they are. That's why soap operas and Oprah Winfrey-type shows are so successful.

Women don't need sex as often as men do. This is because sex is more physical for men and more emotional for women. Just knowing that the man *wants* to have sex with them fulfils the emotional need.

Women hate bugs. Even the strong-willed ones need a man around when there's a spider or a wasp involved.

Women can't keep secrets. They eat away at them from the inside. And they don't view their gabbing as being untrustworthy, providing they only tell two or three people.

Women always go to public toilets in groups. It gives them a chance to gossip.

Women can't refuse to answer a ringing phone, no matter what she's doing.

Women never understand why men love toys. Men understand that they wouldn't need toys if women had an 'on/off' switch.

Women think all beer is the same.

Women keep three different shampoos and two different conditioners in the shower, as well as at least 10 sundry items.

After a woman showers, the bathroom will smell like a tropical rain forest.

Women don't understand the appeal of sports. Men seek entertainment that allows them to escape reality. Women seek entertainment that reminds them of how horrible things could be.

If a man goes on a seven-day trip, he'll pack five days worth of clothes and will wear some things twice; if a woman goes on a seven-day trip she'll pack 21 outfits because she doesn't know what she'll feel like wearing each day.

Women brush their hair *before* bed.

Watch a woman eat an ice-cream cone and you'll have a pretty good idea about how she'll be in bed.

Women have better restrooms. They get the nice chairs and red carpet.

The average number of items in a typical woman's bathroom is 437. A man would not be able to identify most of these items.

Women love cats. Men say they love cats, but when women aren't looking, men kick cats.

Women love to talk on the phone. A woman can visit her girlfriend for two weeks, and upon returning home, she will call the same friend and they will talk for three hours.

A woman will dress up to go shopping, water the plants, empty the rubbish, answer the phone, read a book, or get the mail.

Women will drive miles out of their way to avoid the possibility of getting lost using a shortcut.

Women do not want an honest answer to the question, 'How do I look?'

PMS stands for: Permissible Man-Slaughter. (Or at least men think it means that. PMS also stands for Punish My Spouse).

The first naked man women see is 'Ken'.

Women are insecure about their weight, bum and breast-size.

Women will make three left-hand turns to avoid making one right-hand turn.

'Oh, nothing,' has an entirely different meaning in woman-language than it does in man-language.

Women cannot use a map without turning the map to correspond to the direction that they are heading.

All women are overweight by definition, don't argue with them about it.

All women are overweight by definition, don't agree with them about it.

If it is not Valentine's Day, and you see a man in a flower shop, you can probably start up a conversation by asking, 'What did you do?'

Women want equal rights, but you rarely hear them clamouring to cover the responsibilities that go with those rights.

Only women understand the reason for 'guest towels' and 'good china'.

Women can get out of speeding tickets by pouting. This will get men arrested.

~~~~~~~~

If marriage were outlawed, only outlaws would have in-laws.

Facts About Men

Men like to barbecue. Men will cook if danger is involved.

Men who have pierced ears are better prepared for marriage. They've experienced pain and bought jewellery.

Marrying a divorced man is ecologically responsible. In a world where there are more women than men, it pays to recycle.

Men are very confident people. Usually they are so confident that when they watch sports on television, they think that if they concentrate they can help their team.

Men love to be the first to read the newspaper in the morning. Not being the first is upsetting to their psyches.

All men look nerdy in black socks and sandals.

The way a man looks at himself in a mirror will tell you if he can ever care about anyone else.

A good place to meet a man is at the dry cleaner. These men usually have jobs and bathe.

Men love watches with multiple functions, preferably ones that have a combination address book, telescope and piano.

Men are sensitive in strange ways. If a man has built a fire and the last log does not burn, he will take it personally.

Men are brave enough to go to war, but they are not brave enough to get a bikini wax.

Men have an easier time buying bathing suits.

Women have two types of bathing suit available to them: depressing and more depressing. Men have two types: nerdy and not nerdy.

Women take clothing much more seriously than men. Men never walk into a party and say 'Oh, my God, I'm so embarrassed; get me out of here. There's another man wearing a black tuxedo.'

Most men hate to shop. That's why the men's department is usually on the first floor of a department store, two inches from the door.

If a man prepares dinner for you and the salad contains three or more types of lettuce, he is serious.

If you're dating a man who you think might be 'Mr. Right,' because he a) got older, b) got a new job, or c) visited a psychiatrist, you are in for a nasty surprise. The cocoon-to-butterfly theory only works on cocoons and butterflies.

When four or more men get together, they talk about sports.

When four or more women get together, they talk about men.

Not one man in a beer commercial has a beer belly.

Men who can eat anything they want and not gain weight should do it out of sight of women.

Getting rid of a man without hurting his masculinity is a problem.

'Get out' and 'I never want to see you again' might sound like a challenge. One of the most effective calls is, 'I love you. I want to marry you. I want to have your children.'

Only men who have worn a ski suit understand how complicated it is for a woman to go to the bathroom when she's wearing a jumpsuit.

Men are self-confident because they grow up identifying with superheros.

Women have bad self-images because they grow up identifying with Barbie.

When a woman tries on clothing from her closet that feels tight, she will assume she has gained weight. When a man tries something from his closet that feels tight, he will assume the clothing has shrunk.

Male menopause is a lot more fun than female menopause. With female menopause you gain weight and get hot flashes. With male menopause you get to date young girls and drive motorcycles.

Men forget everything; women remember everything. That's why men need instant replays in sports. They've already forgotten what happened.

Men would like monogamy better if it sounded less like monotony.

All men would still really like to own a train set.

Fun Things To Do in a Public Toilet

Compliment people on their shoes.

Introduce yourself to the person in the next cubicle.

Strike up a conversation.

Provide 'strenuous' sound effects.

Ask the person in the next stall if there's anything swimming in *their* bowl.

Discuss the pros and cons of laxatives.

Scream 'Oh my God! What the hell is that?'

Simulate a drug deal.

Pretend to fall in (with appropriate sound effects).

Roll Easter eggs under the doors.

Start a sing-a-long.

Knock on the doors of occupied stalls and ask if there is anyone in there. If so, ask if they are busy.

Masquerade as a door-to-door salesman.

Ask loudly, 'When does the movie start?'

Write 'nerdy' graffitti like 'Please wash your hands. Thank you.'

Kick in cubicle doors, camera in hand.

Pour water over the cubicle door onto occupant.

Say, 'Oops missed' while syringing water out around the bowl and under the walls and door into other stalls.

Fake an orgasm.

At night, switch off the lights.

Run around naked, yelling 'Where's the fish?'

Collect a door charge.

Ask, in a small, trembling voice, 'Is there a doctor in the house?'

Impersonate Elvis. Be convincing.

Write essay questions on the toilet paper.

Put Glad Wrap over the toilet bowl.

Offer refreshments.

Replace rolls of toilet paper with rolls of sand paper.

Electrify metal urinals.

Leave a ladle in the toilet bowl.

Remove cubicle doors.

Glue seat and cover down to bowl.

Place signs warning of 24-hour video surveillance.

Make cubicle doors lockable only from the outside.

Put itching powder on the toilet seats.

Leave a fried egg floating in the bowl.

Replace soap in dispenser with custard.

Completely soak the towel in the towel dispenser, or the paper towels if available.

Make kitty litter trays that fit into toilet bowls. Install.

Replace condoms in vending machine with tampons (or vice versa).

Create a crime scene complete with police tape and chalk silhouette.

~~~~~~~~~

If it weren't for me, there'd just be a pile of my clothes on the floor.

Travel Agent Translations

Travel Agent Term	Translation
Old world charm.	Room with a bath.
Tropical.	Rainy.
Majestic setting.	A long way from town, at end of dirt road.
Options galore.	Nothing is included in the itinerary.
Secluded hideaway.	Directions to locate unclear.
Some budget rooms.	Sorry, already occupied.
Explore on your own.	At your own expense.
Knowledgeable trip hosts.	They've flown in an aeroplane before.
No extra fees.	No extras.
Nominal fee.	Outrageous charge.
Standard.	Sub-standard.
Deluxe.	Barely standard.
Superior accommodations.	One complimentary chocolate, free shower cap.
All the amenities.	Two chocolates, two shower caps.
Gentle breezes.	In hurricane alley.

Light and airy.   No air conditioning.

Picturesque.   Theme park nearby.

24-hour bar.   Ice cubes at additional cost
                        (when available).

Working in the New Millennium

Cleaning up the dining area means getting the fast food bags out of the back seat of your car.

Your reason for not staying in touch with family is that they do not have email addresses.

You have a 'to do list' that includes entries for lunch and bathroom breaks and they are usually the ones that never get crossed off.

Pick-up lines now include a reference to liquid assets and capital gains.

You consider overnight mail to be painfully slow.

Your idea of being organised is multiple coloured post-it notes.

Your grocery list has been on your refrigerator so long some of the products don't even exist any more.

You lecture the neighbourhood kids selling lemonade on ways to improve their profitability.

You get all excited when it's Saturday so you can go to work in casual clothes.

You refer to the tomatoes grown in your garden as deliverables.

You find you really need Power Point to explain what you do for a living.

You normally eat out of vending machines and at the most expensive restaurant in town within the same week.

You think that 'progressing an action plan' and 'calendarising a project' are acceptable English phrases.

You know the people at the airport hotels better than your next-door neighbours.

You ask your friends to 'think out of the box' when making Friday night plans.

You think Einstein would have been more effective had he put his ideas into a matrix.

You think a 'half day' means leaving at five o'clock.

~~~~~~~

Insanity is hereditary – you get it from your kids.

Things You May Be Overheard Saying in the Darkroom

Hey hey, careful with that thing.

You can't expose it to the light.

Is it stiff yet?

Don't open the door.

I can't get it in.

How much time is left?

I just can't enlarge it to that size.

Would you like to see my exposures?

Don't go anywhere, we're not finished yet.

Use the bath to get rid of the slime.

So how does it go in there?

It doesn't work the way you say.

Check the chart.

I always prefer manual enlarging.

〜〜〜〜〜

Ever stop to think, and forget to start again?

The 10 Commandments of the Frisbee

1. The most powerful force in the world is that of a frisbee straining to get under a car.

2. The better the catch the worse the re-throw (aka 'good catch, bad throw').

3. One must never precede any manoeuvre by a comment more predictive than, 'watch this!'

4. The higher the costs of hitting any object the greater the certainty it will be struck.

5. The best catches are never seen.

6. The greatest single aid to distance is for the frisbee to be going in the wrong direction (aka 'goes the wrong way, goes a long way').

7. The most powerful hex words in the world of sport are: 'I really have this sussed – watch' (aka 'know it, blow it').

8. In any crowd of spectators at least one will suggest that razor blades could be attached to the frisbee.

9. The greater your need to make a good catch the greater the probability your partner will deliver his worst throw.

10. The single most difficult move with a frisbee is to put it down (aka 'just one more throw').

Laws of Documentation

1. If it should exist, it doesn't.

2. If it does exist, it's out of date.

3. Only documentation for useless programs transcends the first two laws.

Laws of Love

People to whom you are attracted invariably think you remind them of someone else.

The love letter you finally got the courage to send will be delayed in the mail long enough for you to make a fool of yourself in person.

The probability of a young man meeting a desirable and receptive young female increases by pyramidal progression when he is already in the company of:
1. a date
2. his wife
3. a better-looking and richer male friend.

Bored in a Lecture at Uni?

Try to develop psychic powers, then use them.
Inflate a beachball and throw it around the room.

Sing showtunes.

Fake a seizure.

Make loud animal noises then deny doing it.

Think of new pick-up lines. See if they work.

Pretend you're flying a jet fighter in the Gulf War.

Churn some butter.

Create a brand new language.

Walls made of brick: count them.

Plot revenge against someone.

Think of nicknames for everyone you know.

Punch the person next to you in the mouth.

See how long you can hold your breath.

Take your pants off and give them to the lecturer.

Chew on your arm until someone notices.

Change seats every three minutes.

Think of ways to cheat at Trivial Pursuit.

Shave.

Run across the room, tag someone and say 'You're it.'

Announce to the class that you are God and that you are angry.

Think of five new ways to use your shoes.

Run to the window, then say, 'Sorry, I thought I saw the bat-signal'.

Ask the person in front of you to marry you.

Start laughing really hard and say, 'Oh, now I get it.'

Make a sundial.

Sell stolen goods.

Bite people.

Summarise the teachings of Socrates in 50 words or less.

Give yourself a new identity.

Write a screenplay about a diabetic Swedish girl who can't swim.

Start a Mexican wave.

Dig an escape tunnel.

Learn voodoo.

Lick yourself clean.

Lick someone else clean.

Learn to tie your shoes with one hand.

See how many push-ups you can do.

Experiment with your sexuality.

Run with scissors.

Write stupid lists.

Space Age Product Warnings

Warning: This product warps space and time in its vicinity.

Warning: This product attracts every other piece of matter in the universe, including the products of other manufacturers, with a force proportional to the product of the masses and inversely proportional to the distance between them.

Caution: The mass of this product contains the energy equivalent of 85 million tonnes of TNT per net ounce of weight.

Handle with extreme care: This product contains minute electrically charged particles moving at velocities in excess of five hundred million kilometres per hour.

Consumer notice: Because of the 'Uncertainty Principle', it is impossible for the consumer to find out at the same time both precisely where this product is and how fast it is moving.

Advisory: There is an extremely small but non-zero chance that, through a process known as 'tunnelling' this product may spontaneously disappear from its present location and reappear at any random place in the universe, including your neighbour's domicile. The manufacturer will not be responsible for any damages or inconvenience that may result.

Read this before opening package: According to certain suggested versions of the grand unified theory, the primary particles constituting this product may decay to nothingness within the next four hundred million years.

This is a 100% matter product: In the unlikely event that this merchandise should contact antimatter in any form, a catastrophic explosion will result.

Public notice as required by law: Any use of this product, in any manner whatsoever, will increase the amount of disorder in the universe. Although no liability is implied herein, the consumer is warned that this process will ultimately lead to the heat death of the universe.

Note: The most fundamental particles in this product are held together by a 'gluing' force about which little is currently known and whose adhesive power can therefore not be permanently guaranteed.

Attention: Despite any other listing of product contents found herein, the consumer is advised that, in actuality, this product consists of 99.9999% empty space.

New grand unified theory disclaimer: The manufacturer may technically be entitled to claim that this product is 10-dimensional. However, the consumer is reminded that this confers no legal rights above and beyond those applicable to three-dimensional objects, since the seven new dimensions are 'rolled up' into such a small 'area' that they cannot be detected.

Please note: Some quantum physics theories suggest that when the consumer is not directly observing this product, it may cease to exist or will exist only in a vague and undetermined state. No responsibility is taken by the manufacturers of the product should this occur.

Component equivalency notice: The subatomic particles (electrons, protons, etc.) comprising this product are exactly the same in every measurable respect as those used in the products of other manufacturers, and no claim to the contrary may legitimately be expressed or implied.

Health warning: Care should be taken when lifting this product, since its mass, and thus its weight, is dependent on its velocity relative to the user.

Important note to purchasers: The entire physical universe, including this product, may one day collapse back into an infinitesimally small space. Should another universe subsequently re-emerge, the existence of this product in that universe cannot be guaranteed.

Laws of Life

It is easier to get forgiveness than permission.

Under the most rigorously controlled conditions of pressure, temperature, volume, humidity, and other variables, the organism will do as it damn well pleases.

Research is what I'm doing when I don't know what I'm doing.

It is not an optical illusion, it just looks like one.

There are two rules for success... 1. Never tell everything you know.

When in doubt, predict that the present trend will continue.

Don't force it; get a larger hammer.

Any tool when dropped will roll into the least accessible corner of the workshop.

An alcoholic is a person who drinks more than his own physician.

If all you have is a hammer, everything looks like a nail.

If you're feeling good, don't worry. You'll get over it.

Project teams detest weekly progress reporting because it so vividly manifests their lack of progress.

Never go to a doctor whose office plants have died.

You always find something in the last place you look.

When in charge, ponder. When in trouble, delegate.

When in doubt, mumble.

If computers get too powerful, we can organise them into a committee – that will do them in.

No good deed goes unpunished.

Whenever a system becomes completely refined, some damn fool discovers something which either abolishes the system or expands it beyond recognition.

Nothing is ever accomplished by a reasonable man.

When all else fails, read the instructions.

You can fool all of the people some of the time, and some of the people all of the time, but you can't fool your mum.

The amount of time required to complete a government project is precisely equal to the length of time already spent on it.

When things just can't possibly get any worse, they will.

Man will occasionally stumble over the truth, but most of the time he will pick himself up and continue on.

All probabilities are 50%. Either a thing will happen or it won't. This is especially true when dealing with someone you're attracted to.

In any organisation, there will always be one person who knows what's going on; this person must be fired.

Virtue is its own punishment.

If you hit two keys on the typewriter, the one you don't want hits the paper.

The first bug to hit a clean windshield lands directly in front of your eyes.

If you view your problem closely enough you will recognise yourself as part of the problem.

Opportunity always knocks at the least opportune moment.

Our chief want in life is somebody who shall make us do what we can. Having found them, we shall then hate them for it.

If you are given an open-book exam, you will forget your book. If you are given a take-home exam, you will forget where you live.

Procrastination avoids boredom; one never has the feeling that there is nothing important to do.

Science is true. Don't be misled by facts.

If an experiment works, something has gone wrong.

No matter what the anticipated result, there will always be someone eager to misinterpret it, fake it, or believe it happened according to his own pet theory.

In any collection of data, the figure most obviously correct, beyond all need of checking, is the mistake.

Once a job is fouled up, anything done to improve it only makes it worse.

A closed mouth gathers no feet.

No matter which way you ride, it's uphill and against the wind.

Procrastination shortens the job and places the responsibility for its termination on someone else (namely the authority who imposed the deadline).

Celibacy is not hereditary.

History doesn't repeat itself – historians merely repeat each other.

The time when you need to knock on wood is when you realise that the world is composed of vinyl, glass and aluminium.

It is usually impractical to worry beforehand about interferences – if you have none, someone will make one for you.

Push something hard and it will fall over.

If you knew what you were doing you'd probably be bored.

An object in motion will always be headed in the wrong direction.

An object at rest will always be in the wrong place.

The energy required to change either one of these states will always be more than you wish to expend, but never so much as to make the task totally impossible.

Investment in reliability will increase until it exceeds the probable cost of errors, or until someone insists on getting some useful work done.

The secret to success is sincerity. Once you can fake that, you've got it made.

If the shoe fits, it's ugly.

Always hire a rich attorney. Never buy from a rich salesman.

If a string has one end, it has another.

You never really learn to swear until you learn to drive.

Anything is possible if you don't know what you're talking about.

Eighty per cent of all people consider themselves to be above-average drivers.

The belief that enhanced understanding will necessarily stir a nation to action is one of mankind's oldest illusions.

Never attribute to malice that which is adequately explained by stupidity.

There are never enough hours in a day, but always too many days before Saturday.

Experience is directly proportional to the amount of equipment ruined.

For every action, there is an equal and opposite criticism.

You can lead a horse to water, but if you can get him to float on his back, you've got something.

The first myth of management is that it exists.

If you have a difficult task, give it to a lazy person – they will find an easier way to do it.

Inside every large problem is a small problem struggling to get out.

Among economists, the real world is often a special case.

Everyone has a scheme that will not work.

The chance of forgetting something is directly proportional to... to... uh...

You can never tell which way the train went by looking at the track.

Everybody lies, but it doesn't matter, because nobody listens.

When the going gets tough, everyone leaves.

The one day you'd sell your soul for something, there's a glut of souls on the market.

When we try to pick out anything by itself, we find it hitched to everything else in the universe.

Cleanliness is next to impossible.

No matter where you go, there you are.

It is a mistake to let any mechanical object realise that you are in a hurry.

On the way to the corner, any dropped tool will first strike your toes.

People who love sausages and respect the law should never watch either one being made.

The correct advice to give is the advice that is desired.

The purpose of the communication is to advance the communicator.

The information conveyed is less important than the impression.

Change is the status quo.

A manager cannot tell if he is leading an innovative mob or being chased by it.

A decision is judged by the conviction with which it is uttered.

To protect your position, fire the fastest rising employees first.

Decisions are justified by the benefits to the organisation, but they are made by considering the benefits to the decision-makers.

Anyone else who can be blamed should be blamed.

Anything that can go wrong will go wrong faster with computers.

Whenever a computer can be blamed, it should be blamed.

In any decision situation, the amount of relevant information available is inversely proportional to the importance of the decision.

You cannot successfully determine beforehand which side of the bread to butter.

Bare feet magnetise sharp metal objects so they always point upwards from the floor – especially in the dark.

A memorandum is written not to inform the reader but to protect the writer.

Trouble strikes in series of threes, but the next job after a series of three is not the fourth job – it's the start of a brand new series of three.

Complaints to the Landlord

Below is a series of complaints sent in by various tenants to their landlords.

I wish to complain that my father hurt his ankle very badly when he put his foot in the hole in his back passage.

The lavatory is blocked; this is caused by the boys next door throwing their balls on the roof.

This is to let you know that there is a smell coming from the man next door.

The toilet seat is cracked: where do I stand?

I am writing on behalf of my sink, which is running away from the wall.

I request your permission to remove my drawers in the kitchen.

Our lavatory seat is broken in half and is now in three pieces.

Can you please tell me when our repairs are going to be done, as my wife is about to become an expectant mother.

I want some repairs done to my stove as it has backfired and burnt my knob off.

I am still having trouble with smoke in my built-in drawers.

The toilet is blocked and we cannot bath the children until it is cleared.

The person next door has a large erection in his back garden, which is unsightly and dangerous.

Will you please send someone to mend our cracked sidewalk? Yesterday my wife tripped on it and is now pregnant.

Our kitchen floor is very damp, we have two children and would like a third, so will you please send someone to do something about it.

Will you please send a man to look at my water, it is a funny colour and not fit to drink.

Would you please send a man to repair my downspout. I am an old age pensioner and need it straight away.

Could you please send someone to fix our bath tap. My wife got her toe stuck in it and it is very uncomfortable for us.

I want to complain about the farmer across the road. Every morning at 5:30 his cock wakes me up, and it is getting too much.

When the workmen were here they put their tools in my wife's new drawers and made a mess. Please send men with clean tools to finish the job and keep my wife happy.

Infamous Last Words

Let it down slowly.

Rat poison only kills rats.

I'll get your toast out.

It's strong enough for both of us.

This doesn't taste right.

I can make this light before it changes.

Nice doggie.

I can do that with my eyes closed.

I've done this before.

Well we've made it this far.

That's odd.

Okay this is the last time.

With those guns, those guys couldn't hit the side of a...

Don't be so superstitious.

Now watch this.

This planet has an atmosphere just like on earth.

What duck?